THE
DAYS
AND THE
SEASONS

Photographer: A. Kühne, Leipzig.

Wayne State University Press   Detroit

THE DAYS AND THE SEASONS

memoirs

EVYATAR FRIESEL

COPYRIGHT © 1996

BY WAYNE STATE UNIVERSITY PRESS,

DETROIT, MICHIGAN 48201. ALL RIGHTS ARE RESERVED.

NO PART OF THIS BOOK MAY BE REPRODUCED WITHOUT FORMAL PERMISSION.

MANUFACTURED IN THE UNITED STATES OF AMERICA.

99 98 97 96   5 4 3 2 1

Library of Congress Cataloging-in-Publication Data

Friesel, Evyatar.
    The days and the seasons : memoirs / Evyatar
Friesel.
        p.   cm.
    Includes index.
    ISBN 0-8143-2635-8 (alk. paper)
    1. Friesel, Evyatar.   2. Jews, German—Israel—
Biography.   3. Jewish historians—Israel—Biography.
4. Holocaust, Jewish (1939–1945)—Germany—
Influence.
    I. Title.
    DS113.8.G4F75   1996
956.9405'092—dc20
    [B]   96-12391

DESIGNER: S. R. Tenenbaum

TO **K.**, WHO BELIEVED IN MIRACLES

The hours, the days and the seasons,
Order their souls aright.

—Rudyard Kipling, "The Recall"

CONTENTS

7

P_{AUSING}

Heidelberg was a city easy to live in. Closed in between green mountains and the river Neckar, the city is small, agreeable, soft. It was the fall of 1989. My way back to Germany had been gradual, slow—indeed, it had taken fifty years.

I was living in Jerusalem, a professor of modern Jewish history at the Hebrew University. My family had left Germany shortly before World War II, when I was eight years old, and settled in Brazil, where I grew up. Later, in the early 1950s, I moved again, to Israel. As happens with so many Israelis, my personal decision had been to integrate into the Jewish state, its new society and new culture. To the extent that I was able to direct my life, I had not been unsuccessful. However, time breeds reflectiveness: one stops running, looks back to reconsider the way travelled. Then the relativity of the effort becomes evident. One discovers again that old truth, that no man controls his own destiny.

Beyond my plans and ambitions, amid the apparent turmoil of Israel, I became aware of belonging to a certain group whose outline I was beginning to grasp. My life had developed in a way

9

not unlike that of other people who had a personal history similar to mine. We had travelled, I came to believe, a way which deserved to be told. Not because we had some message that was so singular. Whatever we had in common, we were, apparently, unable to utter it with a common voice. My generation is a group of strangely disparate individuals.

I thought that ours was a story that should be known, for behind the tales—mine, others'—I discerned the contour of the human condition. Beyond being the description of a one-time situation, that of a certain generation maturing around the years of World War II, it was perhaps a tale with a broader significance, with a glimmer of things-to-come, apt to repeat itself, to become a general way, a general fate.

∾

Heidelberg was a city easy to live in. I had come for a year, to teach at the Hochschule für Jüdische Studien, an institution for higher Jewish studies connected with Heidelberg University. Here I was then, in the country of my childhood, from which we had escaped in 1939. Why had I returned? Certainly because of my academic work in modern Jewish history, but more particularly because of my wish to understand the troubled German-Jewish chapter of that history. Occasional meetings I had had with Germans in Israel or in the United States had left an odd impression. In many cases the contact had been surprisingly easy and positive. I wanted to know more, and directly, about Germany and about Germans.

Further, there was something like a personal urge, although I had trouble defining it: impressions from my earlier life had begun to arise in my mind, certain memories, certain blurred images from years ago. Like phantoms, they passed occasionally through my consciousness. Were they trying to tell me something? Were they trying to direct me somewhere—or away from something?

1

German Overture

Could it have been Nuremberg, in September 1934 or 1935? We had arrived at a large camp, filled with what seemed an overwhelming number of people. There were no chairs; everybody stood. A large dais, covered with Nazi flags and symbols, dominated one end of the camp. I remember the slow ascent of the uniform-clad dignitaries to the dais, the rhythmic shouting of the crowd—"Sieg Heil! Sieg Heil!"—the hands raised in the Nazi salute. Then everybody stood silent. Somebody—I think it was Adolf Hitler—spoke, his voice booming over the plain.

One of my early indelible childhood recollections is participating in that Nazi mass meeting. I was four or five years old. My mother, my infant twin sisters, Ruth and Edith, and I had been spending the summer away from home. The owner of the house we were staying in took me to the gathering the Nazis were staging nearby. I was bored: there were no other children to play with. The main impression the event left on me was the silence and the orderliness of that huge crowd, listening immobile for what to me seemed endless hours.

Although Nazi-related matters occupied a significant place in my younger years, I remember that period as one of personal happiness. We lived in Chemnitz, a medium-sized town in Saxony, an industrial center of some importance. My parents were of Eastern-European origin and had arrived in Germany separately. The garment business they owned in Chemnitz was doing quite well. By the late 1930s they enjoyed a very comfortable economic situation, and for this reason they remained in Germany until quite late. Only after "Kristallnacht," the night between the ninth and tenth of November 1938, when the synagogues in Chemnitz and elsewhere were burned down and the windows of Jewish shops (including ours) were broken, did my parents decide that time was up.

"Kristallnacht" I remember well. My parents' business was on the second floor, and our living quarters were adjacent. When I woke in the morning I found the large shop windows broken, destroyed by bricks hurled from the street below. Two big Nazi storm-troopers, SA men, had come up to the second floor and were addressing my apprehensive parents in loud voices. Later I went out. It was a cold morning. Here and there I saw broken shopwindows, in buildings I had not know belonged to Jews. I arrived at the main synagogue, a building I remember as large and beautiful, built of red brick. Only the external walls remained. Smoke still rose from behind the walls. People stood, stared silently—very silently—then moved away. It was cold, very cold.

As I came to understand only much later, our home was arranged rather peculiarly. Both my parents were much occupied with their flourishing business and my mother with caring for my little sisters. Because our apartment and my parents' shop were on the same floor, our family life was close and cozy. Once I had reached a certain age, I lived in our shop as much as in our home. It was there, on my father's desk in the small office, that I read the newspaper or did my homework, at least when things were quiet. I attribute my later habit of doing most of my work at home—with my children around me in my studio, rather than in my office at the university—to that early custom of working in my parents' shop. Actually, it was a pattern of life with deeper roots. In 1937 I was taken to visit my mother's home, in Szendiszow, a small town in Western Galicia.

Her family had a garment business, too (with many similar items), and the living arrangements were like ours: the shop in the front, the living quarters in the back, the children going back and forth, everything integrated. The difference was the much greater size of the home and business in Chemnitz.

On Saturdays, matters in my parents' shop became hectic. This was the main business day of the week, when farmers would come in from the countryside to buy suits or coats. There was additional staff to deal with the veritable crowd that sometimes filled the place. When dinnertime came, the maid would take care of my sisters, but I soon developed my own arrangements. I would wait quietly at the door of the busy shop until my mother noticed me. She knew what I wanted: thirty pfennig, to eat out! I was probably no more than five or six when I started having a light Saturday evening dinner in one or another of the nearby eating places, where I became a well-known, hungry and happy customer.

Originally my first name was Siegfried. It was typical for Jewish immigrants from Eastern Europe to give their children Germanic names. Apparently this was an expression of their hopes regarding their future in the country. Later, when I arrived in Israel, I changed my name to Evyatar. This was a mistake. It sounds artificial to me to this day, and people close to me call me Sigi.

In general, my childhood was endowed with that most precious of formative conditions: personal freedom. I remember to this very day the happy sense of independence I felt then. I believe that a great deal of the self-reliance, whether in behavior or in intellect, I may have shown later in life stems from the relative freedom I enjoyed during the first eight years of my existence. From a very early age I also had a "personal means of transportation": a scooter. I travelled over the whole city with it.

I wonder if some of the problems I encountered once I started school were not, after all, a blessing in disguise. I attended Heinrich Beck Schule, a regular elementary school. I was one of two Jewish boys in the class, and we had to sit in the back of the room. Herr Forster, the teacher, was a proud member of the Nazi party and openly antisemitic. Although I had little contact with my Christian classmates, I do not remember hearing antisemitic remarks from them or receiving other abuse because we were Jewish. I enjoyed the reading and writing lessons, and was soon reading. I had trouble, however, with gymnastics: as part of the regimen, we—six-year-old children—were taught to march. I simply could not grasp what Herr Foster wanted, what he meant by his "one-two-left/one-two-left" orders.

On the whole, it seems that I rather "disconnected" from the classroom atmosphere and lived in my own world. Interestingly, the teacher, obviously a professional, seemed to have grasped the situation. On my report card, where most of my grades were only "average," he mentioned my absentmindedness, yet he added that when properly stimulated I was able to produce good results.

In fact, I was continuing the rather free life of my preschool days. I loved to spend time in the large department stores, Tietz and Schocken, which were filled with people and merchandise. Those stores were owned by Jews, and I still remember the impression of the broken windows at the Tietz store after Kristallnacht. Now, in the late 1930s, there were frequent incidents with street rowdies, who knew about my Jewishness. I gave as good as I got, but it was a situation where the odds were against me. Twice I ended up at the doctor's, to have stitches sewn in my upper lip and later my brow.

Shortly after the start of my second year at the Heinrich Beck Schule, all Jewish kids were expelled. The Jewish community attempted some provisional arrangements for their children, setting up classes where youngsters of diverse ages were supposed to study together. I remember this arrangement as crowded and rather confused, and after some months it came to an end. The teacher, "Herr Elend" (misery, in English), "hatt sich um die Ecke gebracht," the elders whispered—i.e., had committed suicide. No other teacher was available. My schooling in Germany was finished.

Several months later, at the beginning of 1939, we left Germany for Brazil. To help keep me occupied during the long sea voyage, I got my first book. It was a fat volume of the stories of the Brothers Grimm. To my parents' surprise, I finished it long before we left. Nevertheless, it served as it was meant to. I read the book again and again. Thus another lifelong habit was born. I continue to reread the books I love, starting in again wherever the book happens to open.

The essential feeling from those German days that is engraved in my memory is not one of fear or anguish, but of curiosity. I cared little about people but found the things and happenings in my day-to-day life highly interesting. Altogether, those were good years—or was it only a later-day impression?

℘

I returned to Chemnitz forty-five years later, in the summer of 1984. Now it was Karl-Marx-Stadt, in East Germany. I was excited: a mixture of objective interest and a strong urge to see again the places of my childhood I had kept in my recollections. The day was warm and windy. The wind added to my commotion. From the railroad station I walked to the center of town. We had lived at Langestrasse 29, the corner of Brettgasse. Brettgasse connected Langestrasse to the Marktplatz, the central square where the municipal building, the Rathaus, stood. I found the Marktplatz and the Rathaus, but nothing else. I asked an old man what had happened to Langestrasse. He told me it had disappeared. The direction of the streets had been altered. The whole city had been destroyed or changed, by war, by men.

The original buildings of the department stores, Tietz and Schocken, still stood, but they had been renamed. The Schocken building was a pearl of German architecture of the 1920s, one of the great works of Erich Mendelsohn. Now it looked dilapidated. I remembered the interior of the store as sumptuous: full of light, filled with goodies. Now it was murky: shabby merchandise, stacks half empty.

I left the store. The wind blew strongly, and that hot wind seemed to connect with some childhood memory I tried to localize, but couldn't. Now I no longer felt either interest or curiosity. I experienced something like fear. I went quickly to the train station—and suddenly it occurred to me that this was the same station we had left from in 1939. Indeed, the same station where my little cousin Margot had been deported from some months earlier. It seemed to me that I was being watched. I wanted to be away, away. I took the first train out. I had been in Chemnitz for less than three hours. Only when I was back in West Berlin did I calm down.

2

Margot

One autumn night in 1938, when I was eight years old, I awoke and found a very strange situation at home. My bed was being moved into a corner, and my room and my parents' bedroom were full of people I did not know. They were sleeping in beds, on the floor, everywhere. The next day I heard that the Gestapo had rounded up all Polish Jews during the night, loaded them on trains and expelled them to Poland. Some had advance notice of the roundup and escaped from their houses before the arrival of the police. Several had sought refuge in my parents' flat: my father had Brazilian citizenship papers and these had protected him from a similar fate. The rigid mind-set of the Nazi organization made it possible for people who had not been taken away to return to their homes the next day: anyone who had not been caught that night was allowed to organize his next steps by himself—obviously, to leave Germany as fast as possible.

My father had not spent the night at home. Among those rounded up by the Gestapo were my uncle Kalman Kugelmas, his wife Hannah—who was my mother's sister—and their daughter Margot, then five years old, the age of my twin sisters. Uncle Kalman had called my father when the police arrived. He went to meet them at the railroad station, where confusion reigned: hundreds of frightened Jews moved back and forth, not knowing what was going to happen.

My father had a proposal: why not leave little Margot with my parents? In all the confusion at the railroad station, nobody would notice if my father took her with him. She was close to my sisters and could blend easily into our family. Why not? My aunt and uncle hesitated. Margot was their only child. Time was short. People were being moved into the trains. Those were excruciating minutes. Their turn arrived. They took Margot with them.

Never in their lives did my parents cease to regret that decision. In their old age, sixty years later, they still suffered over it as if it had happened the day before.

We left Germany several months later, at the beginning of 1939. In March 1939 we arrived in Brazil. One of the first steps my parents took there was to try to get the Kugelmases out of Poland. Procedures were slow and complicated. The German invasion of Poland, in September 1939, caused new difficulties. Nevertheless, in the winter of 1939–40, my father managed to have visas to Brazil waiting for them at the Brazilian embassy in Warsaw. The Kugelmases left Szendiszow, the village where they were staying with my mother's family, and boarded the train to Warsaw, a day's travel from the village. It was bitterly cold, and the train was unheated; there was danger of freezing to death during the journey. They decided to return to Szendiszow. They never made it to Warsaw.

I had been to Szendiszow with my mother in 1937, to visit her family. From there we had traveled to Przemysl, on the border between Eastern and Western Galicia, where my father's family lived. It was my only opportunity to meet my two grandmothers, my uncles, aunts and cousins. There was also an uncle, Itzhak, my father's brother, who later received us in Paris, on our way to Brazil. They all perished in the Holocaust, the whole family, on both sides.

The Holocaust has always had for me a broad and general meaning, a deeply felt tragedy of the whole Jewish people. In the ambit of my professional work I have studied its origins— and tried to understand its consequences. With the years, I have become more and more sensitive to my parents' permanent anguish over that fateful decision, taken on that night in October 1938, concerning little Margot. Her destiny, evoking the terrible casualness of life and death, has become, more than anything else, my personal symbol of the Holocaust.

3

My Parents

     My parents were typical Eastern European Jews. Both had been born in Galicia, which was part of the Austro-Hungarian Empire before World War I and later became part of Poland. Ours was, then, a family of "Galitzianer," and this molded my character deeply. Galician Jews, with their peculiar mix of shrewdness and heartiness, are the Jewish ethnic group I feel most at home with. When, much later in life, I came back to Germany, it became obvious to me that while I understood Germans quite well, I "functioned" differently than they did.

     My father, Joseph Berr Friesel, had served in the Austro-Hungarian army during World War I. Days after his demobilization at the end of the war, and the subsequent collapse of the Hapsburg Empire, he was summoned to enlist again, this time in the Polish army. The last thing he wanted was to be caught up in the vicious war going on in the Polish-Russian borderlands. He escaped from the country and emigrated to Brazil.

     In Brazil my father found himself once again in the military, this time in the Brazilian navy. He remained in Brazil until 1924, when a revolution broke out in São Paulo, where he was trying to establish a business. Fed up with wars and army service, he decided to return to Europe, to Germany. In Chemnitz he met my future mother, Bluma Bloner, or Blauner.

My father, who in his old age remained lucid and in relatively good health, would tell me about strange happenings in his younger years. About battles he had participated in during World War I, where he became lost in the fog and the confusion and survived, while his battalion was wiped out. Or about a period spent in the Brazilian navy in the early 1920s, when he was called the "German sailor." This brief Brazilian period in his life saved our family in the Nazi era, because, as mentioned before, my father adopted Brazilian nationality before returning to Germany.

My father told his story in a matter-of-fact way; he was not a man for much introspection. Indeed, only when I became an adult did I realize that the real brains in our family were my mother's—who also lived into her nineties, mentally sharp until the end. Even the business they owned in Germany had been my mother's. She opened it before she married my father, and had done well on her own. As happened to so many women of her generation, she accepted submissively—but never gladly— her traditional role in a Jewish family led by a rather authoritarian husband. It took me years to recognize that my father, a man of steady character, trustworthy and hardworking, was not endowed with a very strong personality. Nor was he especially intelligent.

However, there was something granitelike about both of them. Theirs was the generation that bore the full brunt of the upheavals that the twentieth century brought upon the Jewish people. Both my parents took it all and hardly flinched. My father changed countries or living conditions five or six times in his life. From his native Galicia to Brazil, after World War I; several years later back to Europe, this time to Germany. Then came fifteen years in Germany, where my parents met, married, prospered and begot three children. Early in 1939 they fled from Germany, again to Brazil, a country my mother did not know and my father had forgotten. They rebuilt their lives there, first in Rio de Janeiro, then in São Paulo, in the 1940s and 1950s. But their children were caught in the whirlwind of Zionism and the creation of the Jewish state: all three emigrated to Israel in the 1950s and built their lives there. Alone in Brazil, totally rootless, my parents ended by emigrating again. In 1962 they settled in Tel Aviv.

It was not the end of their journey, however. In the late 1970s they moved once more, this time to kibbutz Bror Hail, where I had been a member in the 1950s, and to which my sister Edith still belonged. For my father, then in his mid-seventies, this turned out to be a significant step. In the kibbutz he began to work again, half-days in the post office. In addition he became responsible for the synagogue and a leading figure in the community of the elders. I remember asking him once, when he was well into his eighties, how he felt, and he answered, "I am much too busy to think about how I feel!"

I never heard my parents complain about their fate or their rootlessness, or grumble about the tours and detours of their lives. They simply accepted things as they were, and did their best to confront each new reality with dignity. Two months before his death in the spring of 1990, at the age of ninety-four, my father was still working in the post office at the kibbutz.

4

Adolescence in Brazil

In March 1939 we arrived in Rio de Janeiro, then the capital of Brazil. I was eight years old. We lived in Rio for about a year, and then we moved to São Paulo, where I remained until 1953, when I emigrated again, this time to Israel.

In the late 1930s Brazil was certainly a much more secure environment for a Jewish child than Germany, where my family and I would not have survived. But in terms of my personal life and development, the situation did not suit me well. In hindsight, more than half a century later, I understand that I never managed to feel at home in Brazil. As much as I immersed myself in Brazilian life and culture—indeed, all my schooling took place there—I never really found ground under my feet. My lack of connection had nothing to do with Brazil as such, that most hospitable country. The problem was my own condition, that of a boy transferred from one habitat to another. This situation repeated itself in my generation again and again, and it happened often that the transition would work well. In my case, it did not. I attribute many of my later psychological difficulties and weaknesses to the changes I experienced in those early years.

At the beginning, my adaptation seemed to go smoothly enough. After several weeks in Rio de Janeiro I started school. I went to the Lycée Française, a culturally French-oriented, good private school in Flamengo, the neighborhood in which we were living. Within several months I had mastered the Portuguese language well enough to participate in class activities. I made friends and came to like Rio very much, as do most people who have an opportunity to live there. Our home was close to the seashore, and we spent much of our free time there.

By the end of 1939 certain business opportunities led my parents to move again, this time to São Paulo, the economic capital of Brazil. We settled there in 1940. At the beginning we lived here and there, until a comfortable flat was found, quite close to the center of the city, where my parents lived until they moved to Israel in 1963.

It was in São Paulo that I lost my direction. I changed schools several times and did not do well in any of them, despite their generally low standards. Neither did I find friends. As a result, I closed myself off within my own inner world. When I was twelve I was forced to repeat a school year, because of my failure in mathematics; I recall that the teacher commented on my illogical approach to quite simple mathematical questions. When I was sixteen I decided to interrupt regular schooling. I convinced my parents—who probably were as baffled about what to do with me as I was myself—that I should enter a technical school and study to become a construction technician.

I finished the three-year course at the Escola Técnica de São Paulo, but most likely more because of the lenient character of the school than because I had developed any talent for the technicalities of the construction trade. In fact, I frequently stayed away from classes. I had discovered the lending section of the municipal library and was reading it, literally, from A to Z. However, in the last year at the technical school two events occurred that affected me directly. I was enrolled in a Portuguese language and literature class whose instructor was a university student, teaching the course as a side-job. One day he came to class without a prepared lecture, and to pass the time he asked us to write an essay on any theme we chose. To his (and my) surprise, I produced a good character profile of someone I knew. Beyond discovering that I had an aptitude for writing, I found that I very much enjoyed the exercise.

The second event happened in the history class I was taking. The teacher, Julio Costa, a man with many social and political connections, had a "straw" job in the school, probably one of several, something that was quite common in the local bureaucracy. In effect, he received a government salary but rarely showed up to teach his class. When he did appear, he told us stories about the diverse revolutions his father and forefathers had participated in. I liked him, and we began to talk together after class. He was smart, a great storyteller, and apparently perceptive, too. At least he recognized that I was in the wrong place. Through political connections Costa arranged for me to try out as a reporter in a newspaper that one of the political parties was just starting in São Paulo. For all intents and purposes, I left the technical school several months before "graduation." By pure chance, I managed to be present at the final examinations, which I somehow passed, with minimal grades. I was eighteen.

5

Newspaper Reporter

Unfortunately, at eighteen I was too immature
to understand the magnificent opportunity that had come my
way through Costa's help, and thus to enjoy it properly. Anyone
who wants to become a writer should spend some time working
for a newspaper, preferably a small one, where the professional
specialization is limited. He will collect enough impressions,
experiences and material to feed his imagination for a lifetime. I
obtained an interview with the *Jornal de São Paulo,* and early one
afternoon I found myself facing Machado, the desk editor responsible for current reporting.

Machado was a cadaverous chain-smoker, pallid, over-
worked. He started his job at 2:30 in the afternoon and finished it at the printing machines, about three o'clock in the
morning. During that time there was always a cigarette in his
mouth. He *was* the newspaper. Machado was in his forties,
but in the eyes of the teenager who stood before him he
looked to be over one hundred years old. As I came to recognize much too late, Machado was a beautiful human being;

modest, helpful and an outstanding example of that precious species, the professional.

On that particular afternoon, however, Machado had a problem: how to get rid of me. It was nothing personal. It was common for political cronies of the editor-in-chief (of whom my sponsor Julio Costa was only one) to recommend hordes of young and not-so-young protegés to begin or to continue a journalistic career with the *Jornal de São Paulo*. What was to be done with them all? Machado was too experienced with Brazilian newspaper realities, and also too tired, simply to throw us out. Instead he gave each bright-eyed newcomer one impossible job: only the fittest would survive. On that particular afternoon, as on most other days, there were several applicants. The fellow ahead of me, a rather obese person a bit older than I, was asked to interview the Cardinal-Archbishop of São Paulo; as he and I discovered later, His Eminence the Cardinal-Archbishop *never* gave interviews.

Machado said my assignment was to go the the Palace of Justice, and to interview the Secretary of Justice about some issue I no longer remember. I went to the impressive Justice Building downtown, entered, went up a large staircase, was directed along what seemed like miles of corridors, and finally arrived at the office of the secretary to the secretary of the Secretary of Justice. I explained what I wanted (of course, I had no credentials proving my "profession" or any introduction from the newspaper). I was asked to wait, and ten minutes later I was escorted into the most sumptuous office I had ever seen, and into the presence of the Secretary of Justice himself.

His Excellence was an extremely dignified looking man in his early sixties, dark-skinned with white hair, handsome. He belonged to one of the old and traditional families of São Paulo. Typically, these families had extensive coffee plantations and were very rich. When I was shown into his office, he was talking on the phone, and he continued his conversation for some time. When I got my bearings and started paying attention to what was going on, it dawned on me, to my total stupefaction, that he was speaking to his mistress. Indeed, he was literally melting over the phone.

Eventually His Excellence finished his conversation, and in obvious high spirits turned to me, offering me a huge cigar (I had never smoked one before and was smart enough not to accept it). He lit one himself and asked, "Now, young man, what can I do for you?" I stated my wish for an interview, black coffee was brought, and we spent the next hour-and-a-half talking together. Nobody bothered us, nobody interrupted. We parted on the best of terms. The Secretary even invited me for lunch, "one of these days," at his home. I was still too inexperienced to understand that he meant it. In the best old Brazilian tradition, the Secretary kept an open house: whoever was invited came and ate. If the host himself was not there, the cook and the maid would look after the guests. One simply entered, asked, " 'tá pronto?" ("is lunch ready?"), and then one would be served an excellent *feijoada*, the Brazilian national dish of black beans and rice.

I went back to the newspaper office to record the interview. Machado looked up at me, surprised to see that I had successfully carried out the assignment. Suddenly there was silence in the large office, where a dozen people had been banging on typewriters. Nobody ever reached the Secretary of Justice for an interview! Later, after I had learned the professional ropes, I never managed again to be admitted into that office. Incidentally, Mello, the rather fat fellow who applied for a job the same afternoon I did, also succeeded—for the first and last time—in gaining admittance into the presence of the Cardinal-Archbishop. We two were the only survivors of a whole crop of hopeful aspirants. Mello later became a well-known journalist.

I typed up the results of my interview and handed them to Machado. He took a look at the piece, through the smoke of his perennial cigarette, and without uttering a word, while I stood in front of his desk, changed it from top to bottom. My apprenticeship in journalism, as well as in the Portuguese language, had begun. This process went on for several months. Machado never said a word of praise or of reproach—he was too busy, too tired, probably too unhappy. From time to time, when he was handing out an assignment, he would make some low-voiced, brief comment or suggestion. I learned to listen carefully: usually it was a gem of professional experience. Six months later, Machado informed me—with that same tired voice and look, cigarette smoke spiraling upward—that I had been promoted to sub-editor. I was totally dumbfounded. I was nineteen.

❧

During that period I came to know and love São Paulo. In the late 1940s the city was completely different from the megalopolis it became ten or twenty years later. In those days São

Paulo had about two million inhabitants. Besides the indigenous population—part white, part black, part mixed—there were many newcomers from other regions of Brazil, especially *nortistas* from the Brazilian northeast. São Paulo derived much of its exotic flavor from the large number of immigrants or children of immigrants, especially Italians, Portuguese and Japanese. The 1920s and 1930s were decades of heavy immigration. By the late 1940s, São Paulo had reached a sociological balance: the majority of immigrants and their descendants had become integrated into the predominant culture, but they still retained many of their original characteristics. In addition, São Paulo was prosperous. It was very similar to another metropolis I came to know later, New York.

As an immigrant myself, I found the atmosphere of São Paulo very congenial: a combination of personal solitude in an environment of work and effort, everyone trying to establish himself, and many indeed succeeding. As a reporter I came to know the city inside out: each one of its neighborhoods, its diverse national and ethnic groups, its economic and political pressure groups, its culture and, connecting it all, the peculiar rhythm of São Paulo, dynamic and optimistic. However, there were corners in that city that gave one pause. For instance, there was a neighborhood I found extremely interesting, although sad. Refugees from the Spanish Civil War had settled there, and lived in great poverty. In the evenings the men (no women ever appeared) met in little bars, humble and darkish, and sat around small tables drinking and smoking. Sooner or later someone produced a guitar. Harsh Andalusian melodies would fill the air already thick with smoke. "Adios Granada, oy Granada mia. . ."—this would go on for hours. They were literally killing themselves, those Spaniards, with alcohol and longing.

ॐ

The daily I worked for was a rough school-of-life, especially for a teenager. It did not take long to grasp that the newspaper, the party it belonged to and most of my co-workers comprised a bunch of crooks, though mostly amiable ones. Interestingly, this was what can only be called "natural" corruption. Corruption was a norm of life and behavior, pervading all other aspects of one's existence, including friendship, loyalty, seriousness in work, even honesty. For instance, most of my colleagues had "straw" jobs: positions in some department of the state, the

federal government (highly regarded, hard to get), or the munici-
pality. In the best cases, they went every day to their public
offices, signed in, and went away. But many did not even do
that. They were nice people, smart professionals, and, in most
cases, good and reliable friends. "But really, Vasco Sigue [my
professional pseudonym], one has to earn an income, right?" I
became convinced and started to look around for a "straw" job
myself. One problem was that at nineteen I was too young to
qualify for a "good" one.

ᘉ

After about two years I became bored with the newspaper
job. A new interest was taking more and more of my time and
attention: the Zionist youth movement. Gradually, the movement absorbed me completely.

6

The Zionist Youth Movement

More than home, school or work environment, the Zionist youth movement finally gave me, the disoriented young man, a social frame and a new direction in life.

The Dror (liberty, in Hebrew) movement was a Jewish pioneer youth organization with a Socialist-Zionist orientation. Youth movements were a typical European phenomenon of the first half of the twentieth century. Although characterized by much inner fervor and personal dedication, these movements never formulated clear aims, and they were easily taken over and misused by totalitarian political regimes. In the case of the Jewish youth movements, Socialist Zionism provided an objective which combined great spiritual intensity with a political goal: pioneering life within the framework of the *kibbutz*, in a newly independent Land of Israel.

Dror was originally established in Poland, in the late 1920s and into the 1930s. Like other Zionist pioneer movements (of which there were many, representing diverse Zionist and socialist tendencies), Dror was brought to South America in the 1930s by Eastern-European Jewish immigrants. The center of its South American activity was in Buenos Aires. Politically it was oriented toward Mapai, one of the main Zionist political parties; this meant it was leftist-moderate. However, those of us in the Brazilian cadre were jealously independent in our ideological orientation, and our socialist positions were more radical than Mapai's. Dror was not the only pioneer youth movement associated with Mapai. There was also Habonim, in the Anglo-Saxon countries; Gordonia, in Europe and later in South America; and Ihud Habonim, established in the 1950s, amalgamating Dror and Gordonia in South America.

The time of the establishment of the State of Israel, from 1947–48, was a period of great enthusiasm among Jews, especially among Jewish youth. Several youth movements sprang up in São Paulo, where the largest Jewish Brazilian community lived. Hashomer Hatzair and Dror were particularly active. Hashomer Hatzair had its own kibbutz movement in Israel, Kibbutz Artzi, and its ideological orientation was farther to the left than Dror's. Both movements were organized throughout the country, with their largest branches in São Paulo, Rio de Janeiro and Porto Alegre, and smaller and less stable groups in several other Jewish communities. In São Paulo, Dror had about 600 members between the ages of ten and twenty. Hashomer Hatzair must have had about the same number, and the smaller movements had altogether another one or two hundred members. In a Jewish community of about thirty to forty thousand, these youth movements were a visible presence, especially since they were highly organized and very active.

The years 1947 to 1955 represent the peak period in the activities of the pioneering youth movements in Brazil. Later, enthusiasm waned and the movements shrank. It was my good fortune that my membership period coincided with the zenith of Dror's activities.

Socialist-Zionism was a very elaborate ideology, in the individual as well as the social sphere. Our goal was the return of the Jews to the Land of Israel, and the establishment there of a socialist commonwealth. The highest, although not the only, expression of that new society was the kibbutz: a community of free women and men where social democracy reigned, private property had been abolished, and the conditions for a society of greater human happiness had been established. Within the framework of the kibbutz, the individual should find fulfillment for his personal capabilities and aspirations.

One of the most significant aspects of Socialist-Zionist ideology was that it had a highly developed personal dimension, as expressed in its social and political goals. A central aim of our movement was the "self-realization" of the individual. This was, undoubtedly, a complex question: what is a "self-realized" individual? In Zionist ideology, "self-realization" related mainly to the ideas of Aharon David Gordon, one of the earlier pioneers and a member of *Kvutza* Degania in the first decade of the twentieth century. Gordon preached the broadening of human consciousness through a complex process of inner regeneration of the individual. The process emphasized renewed contact between the Jew and his Land. Through work, physical agricultural work, a renewed and deeper connection would develop between man and land, and consequently between man and his community, his nation—even between man and God.

Although the kibbutz was a self-contained and relatively independent social unit, its inhabitants understood that its far-reaching social and political aims could be attained only within the framework of broader institutions. The kibbutzim in Palestine were organized into federations, according to different ideological orientations. Together with other rural cooperative organizations and the urban working class, those federations participated in large-scale institutions, such as the Zionist movement and the *Histadrut*, the General Organization of the Jewish Workers in the Land of Israel. In its better years, the Histadrut was a phenomenon as interesting as the kibbutz movement. It adopted many functions of a governmental nature, without being or aspiring to be the state. It seemed the closest one could get, in modern society, to the classical anarchist dream: state-like institutions without the state philosophy typical of nineteenth-century European political thought.

ल

My parents were Zionists, subscribing to a natural kind of Zionism typical of Eastern-European Jews, one that did not need much ideological explanation. My father was the treasurer of the local Zionist organization. Zionist meetings and activities were part of our life and of the lives of most of our acquaintances. It was only normal that I should join a Zionist youth organization, and soon my younger sisters did, too.

I became a member of the Dror organization in 1948, when I was eighteen. The movement had a democratic structure; officers were elected and controlled by a yearly convention. Dror had both local and national activities. Most of the work took place in small cells, *kvutzot*, of about twelve to twenty members each, who were grouped by age. In the summer there were camps, where members from across the country had a chance to meet each other. In the 1950s, both Dror and Hashomer Hatzair maintained small farms outside town. Here the older members, prior to their *aliyah* (emigration) to Israel spent a year, getting used to life in a collective social environment and inured to physical work. The farms were like *kibbutzim:* everybody worked, there was no private property, and the community was democratic and self-reliant.

My activities in Dror gradually came to occupy most of my time. Dror had its national bureau in São Paulo—to which I belonged during the two and a half years before I went to Israel—and I was responsible for the educational work of the movement. The aim of Dror was to transform its members from a disorganized group of pupils and students into a commune of future kibbutz activists. It was a difficult process, involving much soul-searching and hard but sober considerations about our future, our personalities, our professional tendencies, our mutual relations, relationships with our parents and with our Jewish environment. We were to prepare ourselves for *aliya*, for a new life under completely different conditions. Many of the members of the movement did not stay the course, some because of general circumstances and some because of personal ones. We developed a keen sense for human characteristics and a finely tuned capacity for personal judgment. We had to make or participate in decisions involving a level of responsibility and seriousness that have rarely occurred again in my life—and we were barely twenty!

It was in the Zionist youth movement that I learned to think properly, to express myself, to communicate convincingly with others and, last but not least, to lead. In the youth movement I found myself again. Much of what I managed to achieve later on is directly traceable to the personal "opening" I underwent in the movement. If I stress today how important a formative influence Dror was in those years, I should add that my case was not exceptional. Everyone who went through a pioneer Zionist organization will agree that his or her personality was significantly shaped by participation in the movement.

Dror was able to attract a seemingly superior segment of the younger Jewish society, a fact that added to our sense of righteousness. Although not every Jewish youngster participated in the movement, we claimed that those who did were the best. Today it is evident to me that it was not so much that we were better, but that our lives were incomparably more intense, responsible and directed to a higher goal, compared with the existences of regular university students of our age group. Indeed, except for certain later periods—for instance, when I was devoted to writing—I rarely knew again such a level of intense living as I experienced in the Dror movement.

As significant as the whole process was for me personally, the movement had interesting, broader implications. The foundation and early expansion of our movement was tied to a central event in Jewish history: the creation of the State of Israel. Furthermore, the movement had its greatest impact on a particular group of young Jews in our community: the hardcore membership of our movement, the leadership and the most committed activists of Dror were mostly, like myself, foreign-born. True, our schooling was taking place in Brazil; we spoke perfect Portuguese and seemed integrated into the general environment. But most of us, or our parents, were immigrants of Eastern-European origin. Some members of the movement belonged to families who came from Western Europe, but they were a minority. And our ideas seemed to have no attraction whatsoever for the so-called "oriental" Jews who lived in Brazil, those whose parents had emigrated from Muslim countries. We were aware of this disparity: we put a great deal of effort into trying to attract Jewish boys and girls of oriental origin to our movement, but without visible success. In sum, the typical Dror member was a middle-class Jewish youngster of Eastern-European origin, living more or less well in the Brazilian environment, but still strongly conditioned by his or her family's origins.

In addition, our movement attracted some uncommon persons, mostly non-Jews. These included a family of devout Protestants, extremely fine people, the Martins. On the basis of religious beliefs they had concluded that they, too, should move to the Holy Land, and they considered doing it within the framework of our movement. We really did not know how to react to the Martins. They participated in our activities for over a year, until gradually it became clear to all of us that the disparities between us in age, aims and background were too deep. We parted good friends.

Frequently members who had close non-Jewish friends brought them to our activities. These Gentiles gradually became integrated into our group, and several actually emigrated with us to Israel. The strangest of these cases was Senda, our Japanese member. Senda was older than us, and even less at home in Brazil than we were. Everyone liked Senda very much. He had had agricultural experience, so he was extremely helpful at our preparation farm. Senda went with us to Israel and was a member of Bror Hail for quite a number of years. Later he took a job at the Japanese embassy in Tel Aviv, where he worked until his retirement. Senda remained in the country for more than forty years, another uncommon Israeli.

The most touching case, as I remember it, was Itzhak Babsky. One day—when I was already living at our preparatory farm, several months before my departure for Israel—a taxi entered through the gates, and from it came an elderly man, two suitcases, and a teenage boy. No one had been expecting them.

"Good afternoon," said the man. "My name is Babsky. This is my son Itzhak. He is sixteen. We live far, far away in the hinterland. There are no Jews there. I want you to take him with you to Palestine."

The boy did not utter a work. As we discovered later, he was a naturally silent type. We were mute as well; indeed, we were speechless, something that happened to us very rarely. After half-an-hour at most, the father departed in the taxi and Itzhak remained. It was, of course, only a trial. We were still too young to know that nothing is more permanent than a temporary arrangement.

The boy was hard to judge. Dark, Brazilian-looking, silent, physically well-developed for his age, strong, good-willed. One characteristic I paid special attention to: he was fearless. He seemed incapable of grasping what it means to be afraid of something. When the time came to leave for Israel, we were still pondering what to do with him. Itzhak went with us.

In Israel it became evident that he was too young to integrate successfully into our group. He and we decided that he should go into the army, although he was still only seventeen. He volunteered for an elite unit of parachutists and became an excellent soldier: silent, strong, good-willed. In mid-1955 there was an incident at Nitzana, at the desert border between Israel and Egypt. Itzhak's unit was sent to attack an Egyptian position. A volunteer was asked for, and Itzhak presented himself. He still did not know what fear meant. A burst of Egyptian machine-gun fire cut him down. He was the first of us to die in battle.

പ

Our ideological and personal commitment to the movement set us on a collision course with the interests of our parents—and with the trends of our Jewish milieu. Most of our parents were of humble origin and rather limited education. They had managed to work themselves into the middle class, and by the late 1940s they had attained a certain level of prosperity. They belonged to that ever-repeating generation of modern Jews whose children were being prepared for the great social and professional leap forward. Their ambition was to see their sons in the universities, preparing themselves for careers as doctors, engineers, lawyers. And here came the pioneer youth movement, undermining all those hopes! The situation was complicated by the fact that most of our parents were good Zionists. Their dedication to Zionist ideals was rooted deep in their own past. They were keenly interested in the success of the Jewish settlement in Palestine. But their own children, to move to Israel? For a (doubtful) future in a kibbutz? It was impossible not to be aware of the contradiction between the realities of Jewish life in our community and our Socialist-Zionist ideals. It was obvious that once one of our members had started university, daily activities would take up more time and interest, and eventually the course of the studies would take him or her away from the pioneering commitment.

In early May 1950, the leadership of the movement and all the older members met for a three-day-long discussion in São Paulo. The leading figure in the deliberations was Bernardo Cymring (later Dov Tsamir). At the end of our deliberations, the consensus was that we should leave the universities and become full-time activists in the movement. We also decided that our younger members should be oriented toward non-academic studies, such as mechanics, carpentry, construction work and nursing—callings that were congruent with our future kibbutz life. And we concluded that from that point on, university studies should be discouraged as incompatible with the aims of Dror.

It was a veritable revolution, and the next weeks and

months were very difficult. Although there were some excep-
tions, most of our older comrades, some of whom were already
in the third or fourth year of medicine or engineering studies,
left the university. There were terrible family scenes, made even
more difficult because both sons and fathers were not insensitive
to each other's feelings and hopes. Some of our members could
not stand the pressure and either continued their studies or left
the movement altogether. On the whole, however, most of us
held on. It should be said, to the lasting credit of our parents,
that almost no irreconcilable splits developed between them and
their children. Furthermore, there was no break between the
Jewish community and the movement.

Other factors than our new Zionist radicalism caused us to
lose members. We were avowed socialists, and, as had happened before in the European movement, the socialist challenge
was a perpetual question for the ideologically conscious among
us. Where, it was asked, was the right place to work for social
and economic change in society? In Israel? Only in Israel? What
about Brazil, with its multiple social problems? We were not
indifferent to the Brazilian dimension in our lives, and at the
time of national elections we put the whole movement at the
disposal of the local socialist party. Since our level of militancy
and organization was very high, we had some effect. But we also
lost some members to the socialist movement itself. In the early
1950s, the secretary-general of our movement, Paul Singer, underwent an ideological crisis which brought him, after much
soul-searching, to leave Dror. I felt it deeply, for we were close
friends. Singer, who later became a distinguished professor of
economics at the University of São Paulo, remained a dedicated
and active socialist throughout his whole life.

∾

From 1950 on, some older members of the movement left
Brazil for Israel each year, after serving a period of preparation
on our farm. Our aim was to establish a kibbutz of our own,
alone or together with some other group of the Dror movement
or with one of the sister movements. Since my services were still
needed in São Paulo, I spent only seven months at the farm
before *aliyah*. In September 1953, I, too, left Brazil, at the relatively ripe age of twenty-three.

7

In Israel—Kibbutz Bror Hail

We arrived in Israel in late October 1953. Ours was a small group of movement leaders whose departure had been postponed for several months because we were still needed in the movement. We travelled by ship from Brazil to France. In Marseilles we boarded the *S. S. Aliyah,* one of the famous Israeli immigrant ships of the early 1950s. The ship was filled with *olim* (Jewish emigrants) from Morocco. To a later, more sophisticated generation, many of my first impressions may sound naive. However, we *were* astonished to see a Jewish ship, small but white and clean, flying a huge Israeli flag. And the Jewish captain, standing on the upper deck, impeccably white-clad, sun-burned and self-assured—well, seen up close, did he not look a bit like my late uncle Itshemehel? And four days later the arrival in Haifa, a Jewish harbor, Jewish police, Jewish confusion. . . .

One particular image from that event has engraved itself in my mind. Those of us with the Dror group left the ship on one gangway, while the Moroccan *olim*, dressed in oriental garb, descended on a parallel gangway. They disembarked, knelt on the wharf, touched the soil with their foreheads and then kissed the soil of the Holy Land. The remembrance of the scene brings tears to my eyes to this day.

For several years now, groups from our movement, usually consisting of about twenty members, had been arriving in Israel. They generally went to an older kibbutz for further training and began their military service. We had intended that after adapting to the country, undergoing further preparation and military training, and welcoming additional comrades from Brazil, we would make a decision regarding a definite settlement for members of our movement. Our small party arrived in Israel after the fourth large group of Dror members and before the fifth large group was scheduled to emigrate.

By the time we arrived in Israel, some decisions had already been taken about the future, and we were kept informed about them. The first plan had been to settle in Mefalsim, a kibbutz in the northern Negev, near the Gaza strip, founded some years before by *halutzim* (pioneers) from the Argentinian Dror movement. The first two groups of our comrades had gone to Mefalsim, but when misunderstandings arose between the Brazilians and the Argentinians, our comrades decided to leave the settlement. Beyond the quarrels, each sister movement was strong enough to establish its own kibbutz.

Our comrades decided to settle in Bror Hail, several miles north of Mefalsim. A Jewish village with this name had existed in the same neighborhood in the time of Rabbi Yohanan ben Zakai, about eighteen hundred years ago. It is told in the Talmud that candlelight at night in Bror Hail indicated that a male child had been born; incidentally, in our time we renewed that custom. The name Bror Hail, meaning "selection of soldiers," was probably associated with the revolt of Bar Kochba against the Romans in the first half of the second century C.E. There was a large Arab village nearby, Brer (obviously an adaptation of Bror). Its inhabitants had fled during the War of Independence, and only the ruins remained.

In 1948, during that war, members of the Habonim movement from Egypt had erected a military position on the lands of Bror Hail. Later a settlement had been built nearby, and kibbutz Bror Hail was founded. However, many of the members of the Egyptian group had left, and the future of the kibbutz had become doubtful. The arrival of the strong Brazilian contingent solved the problem. When my group and I came to Bror Hail, our comrades had been there for almost a year. On the whole, they had developed good relations with the somewhat older Egyptian founders. Bror Hail was on its way to growing, gradually, into a medium- to large-size kibbutz.

∾

My first weeks in Israel were a succession of impressions that failed to add up to a clear picture. The most practical (which meant cheapest) way to travel through the country was to visit one's relatives or the relatives of one's friends in succession. I went to Tel Aviv, which left me rather unimpressed, and to Jerusalem, which seemed strange—very strange. The only clear idea I formed was that I should come again. I went also to Nahariyah, a small town on the northern seashore, which looked pretty. My most vivid impression from that first trip was of the Jordan Valley and the Kinneret, the Sea of Galilee. The unique beauty of the landscape, with the old and well established settlements around it, was irresistible. By chance I found myself in the little cemetery on the shore of the lake, near *Kvutza* Kinneret. The founding fathers of the Zionist-Socialist movement were buried there: Nachman Syrkin, Ber Borochow, Moses Hess, as well as the great Berl Katznelson, the poetess Rahel, and many others. It was an enchanted corner to which I would return again and again.

For me Bror Hail was rather an anti-climax. For one reason or another I had not so far learned any Hebrew. Back problems made it difficult for me to start working in one of the agricultural branches of the kibbutz. All my life I have enjoyed good health. The only time I have been ill was during my beginnings in Israel. I had been there for about three months when I developed a severe case of pleuritis. I had to be transported to the hospital in Beer Sheva, where I remained for over a month.

Bad as it was, there were some benefits from my stay in the small Hadassah Hospital that existed then in Beer Sheva: I had there my first insight into the great human variety of Israeli society. The Jewish community I had known during my youth in São Paulo was quite uniform. Except for smaller groups that kept to themselves (the Syrian and German Jews), most São Paulo Jews were from Eastern Europe, mainly from Poland and Rumania. They had mostly come from the lower-middle class. In Brazil they had established themselves as small businessmen and slowly attained a modest prosperity. Their adaptation to Brazilian culture was only partial. Most spoke Portuguese poorly, with a strong foreign accent.

In the Beer Sheva hospital I shared a small room with three other men. Two were Jewish types I had never met before. One was an Orthodox Jew, a *hasid*, from a village near Beer Sheva. The man was kind and friendly, but very strict in his religious observances, from morning to evening, day after day, and especially on *shabbat*. My parents were fairly religious, but it was the first time I had lived so close to a totally observant Jew. I noted how effortless his way of life was, in spite of his precise observance of the Law. Interesting, too, was the fact that we other three occupants of the room—two of us completely non-religious kibbutz members— also lived with him effortlessly. Not only did his devoutness not bother us, we felt quite comfortable with it. After all, how far were we from a similar way of life? One generation? Two?

The hospital orderly was a Kurdish Jew, dark and physically powerful. As was not uncommon in Kurdistan, he was married to two wives, and boasted, between both, of twelve children (so far). In Israel, the Jewish Agency people, after much head-scratching, had given him two adjacent flats, one for each wife and her brood. He would stay two weeks with one wife, then two weeks with the other. The way he told it, it was a harmonious arrangement. Yet we had trouble understanding how it worked.

In the room next to ours there was a Bedouin, tall and black, the son of one of the leading sheiks of the Negev region. The father came to visit him frequently, and what a spectacle it was! The sheik was a large man of very dignified behavior, clad in traditional Bedouin garb. He was driven to the hospital in a huge, black, American car (a rarity in Israel in those days), accompanied by two or three armed bodyguards (also his sons).

Most interesting of all was my neighbor. I had arrived at Beer Sheba in rather poor condition, feverish and in pain. "Main nomen iz Efim" (my name is Efim), my new neighbor told me in Lithuanian Yiddish, upon discovering that I hardly knew any Hebrew. He was all attention and kindness. Efim was in his early forties. He had been born in the region of Lithuania that was part of Poland between the world wars. He had been active in the Jewish socialist movement, the Bund. Trapped by the Nazi invasion, he had been sent to one of the large Polish ghettos, from where Jews were later sent to the extermination camps. The Bund had soon organized Jewish resistance in the ghetto.

They had broken out of the city, taken refuge in the woods, and formed a group of guerrilla fighters, partisans. Efim had fought with the Jewish partisans for four years, until the Soviet army reconquered Poland.

Although the Bund was fiercely anti-Zionist, Efim himself had always had a certain interest in Palestine, and he found similar thoughts among members of his partisan unit. With the end of the war, the catastrophe of European Jewry, the destruction of the Bund, Zionism was in effect the only political way that remained open. Efim and his friends had become members of Hashomer Hatzair, the pioneer movement whose socialist ideology was then as extreme as the Bund's. Efim had fought in the illegal immigration movement, trying to break the British sea blockade against the Jews in Palestine. Once in Israel, he had entered a Hashomer Hatzair kibbutz in the Negev and fought again, this time in the War of Independence. By the end of the 1940s, Efim had behind him almost ten uninterrupted years of war—against the Germans, the British, and the Arabs. Now he was sick, with a form of asthma the doctors did not know how to treat. He had long coughing attacks which left him exhausted and breathless, unable to eat or talk.

Efim was a true support, always ready to help and encourage. It was a pleasure to talk with him: he had an excellent Jewish education and spoke beautiful Yiddish. He was well versed in Yiddish literature—about which I knew very little— had a great intellectual curiosity and was extremely open-minded. He was an example of that rare human phenomenon, a man whom hard experience had made better, not worse.

Only much later, when as a result of my studies I learned about that great creation of Eastern-European Jewry, the Jewish labor movement, did I understand Efim better. I would meet men and women with a similar background and mentality: the broad Jewish culture of a secular character, the openmindedness, the commitment to Jewish causes, the militant attitude toward other segments of Jewish society, especially the "clericals." Was it not surprising how well Efim and our *hasid* companion in the hospital room lived together? It was not. As I would discover, relations in Israeli society between striving political parties and spiritual movements were one thing, relations between individual Jews were yet another.

I would also learn later to recognize the tragedy of the Jewish labor movement. In spite of their violent quarrels, the

Bund and the parallel Socialist-Zionist movement had produced Jewish types that were quite similar: good Jewish roots; an excellent Jewish education in Yiddish, Hebrew or both; a secular outlook upon the Jewish and the general world; and, especially, a nobility of mind and pureness of soul that were all the more admirable, considering the difficult conditions in which the movements and their members existed. Efim was the incarnation of all those qualities.

Historical circumstances had beaten the Jewish labor movement. The Bund lost its independence and much of its identity as a result of the Soviet Revolution in 1917. Many of its remaining activists were eliminated during purges in the Soviet Union in the late 1930s. The Polish branch had survived, and was extremely active in Jewish life there, between the world wars. It had been practically liquidated during the Holocaust. The smaller branches that were established in the new concentrations of Jewish emigrés in Western Europe and the Americas had not survived the changing conditions of Jewish life there. Only the Zionist-Socialists in Palestine were successful, up to a point.

After five long weeks I left the hospital. Efim remained, for his condition was getting worse. He died three months later. At the end, I was told, he weighed less than ninety pounds.

I came back to Bror Hail thin, weak and rather dispirited. Soon after my return, personal tensions developed between me and my closer comrades in the kibbutz. There was clearly a significant psychological element in the difficulties I was experiencing. Again I had emigrated, again I was starting life from the beginning. We all were, and this did not make for much mutual patience. Formerly a self-assured, responsible and articulate youth movement leader, I now found myself in a situation where I could not work—an essential activity in a kibbutz society—understood neither the language nor the country, and was losing the social support that might have helped me overcome these difficulties. The fact that I never considered any alternatives besides *aliyah* and kibbutz did not make matters easier.

I sought and tried several solutions, but by the fall of 1954 I decided to take a leave of absence from Bror Hail. To return to Brazil, as several of our members did, never occurred to me, either then or later. The moment I disembarked from that ship I had become an Israeli, period.

The process of leaving the kibbutz—which also meant leaving the movement and the human group I had become a part of—was slow and painful. In retrospect, however, if I had to leave, I chose the best possible time, before I became fully integrated into the kibbutz and assumed tasks and responsibilities. What I could not know then was that I was leaving at a time when the kibbutz movement itself was undergoing significant transformations. Until the establishment of the state, the kibbutz and the pioneer movement associated with it had helped to spearhead the developing Jewish community in Palestine and the effort toward political independence. In spite of the modest size of the kibbutz movement, its members held many key positions in Palestine's Jewish community, as well as in the state after its establishment: in the government, in the army, in the leading institutions.

However, once the State of Israel was created the situation gradually changed. For reasons embedded in the sociology of twentieth-century Jewish society, the kibbutz movement failed to attract any significant part of the mass *aliyah* that came to Israel from Muslim countries after 1948. We all did our best to understand and contend with this failure. The first ideological seminar in which I participated in Israel dealt with that issue. All of us at the conference were aware that socialist Zionism, that complex evolution in Zionist ideology behind the kibbutz movement, reflected the character and aspirations of certain sectors of Eastern-European Jewish society (or, as in our case, the first generation of Eastern-European immigrants in South America). Zionism in Muslim countries had its own content: it was apocalyptic and messianic, deeply imbued with Jewish historical tradition. The particular brand of socialism adopted by Eastern-European Zionism evoked no response from so-called "oriental" Jews. The collective agricultural commune, the kibbutz—which by any standard, Jewish or other, was a very sophisticated social experiment—was too far removed from the life concepts or aspirations of Jewish society in Muslim lands. Another obstacle mentioned at the seminar was the fact that oriental Jews were coming to Israel in overwhelming numbers, thus taxing the Zionists' capacity to integrate them into the kibbutz culture. Additionally, the Jewish pioneer movement was extremely radical and, as such, necessarily elitist. It sought Jewish youth, and was never intended to appeal to Jewish society in general.

This last point struck me forcefully. I recalled the lack of ideological communication with oriental Jews we had experienced while we were still in Brazil. We had failed to attract boys and girls from the oriental part of the Jewish community there, although we had tried very hard. Apparently the historical evolution and situation of diverse Jewries in the twentieth century established a bridge, or failed to establish one, between each group and the kibbutz movement.

Even before the creation of Israel, much of Jewish life there was concentrated in the cities, where most Jews lived. The presence of the pioneering movement was principally evident in the leadership of Jewish life and institutions in what was then Palestine. In the 1950s that leadership was moving to the growing urban centers of the new state. However, it is difficult to exaggerate the formative influence the pioneer movement exerted on Israeli society. I recall that on one occasion in the 1970s, a group of us at the Hebrew University calculated that eighty percent of the professors of our generation had a Socialist-Zionist past, had been activists in the youth movement or kibbutz members. But in the next academic generation the proportion dropped drastically. Although the kibbutz movement was still a phenomenon of high social significance, it was no longer a spearhead of Israeli society.

○

As I have said, I could not have foreseen these historical developments when, in 1954, I decided to look for a new direction for myself, outside the kibbutz and the movement. My last responsibility at Bror Hail was to write a book, in Portuguese, about the Dror movement and Bror Hail. I did this in thirty days, working practically day and night. Published a year later, it was a token of the closing of a personal period, a kind of parting gift to the social group I had lived with for the last five years, and to whom I owed so much.

○

Now, what was I to do, and where should I go? In terms of a profession, I had continued to think about agriculture. Somehow I came upon the idea of forest management. I liked trees, and reforestation was an important national issue. Most of the reforestation in Israel was done by the Keren Kayemet Le'israel, the Jewish National Fund, one of the national institutions of the Zionist movement. The main offices of the KKL were in Jerusalem.

I went to Jerusalem, entered the reforestation department of the Keren Kayemet Le'israel, and with the casualness of the innocent explained, in my still limited Hebrew, that I had come from the Negev (the south) and wanted to work with trees. By chance, the professional agronomist in charge of KKL reforestation in the southern part of Israel happened to be in the office. Yossef Kaplan was a large man, then in his mid-thirties, with big, wise eyes. He looked at me thoughtfully. I remember well the long moment of reflective silence, his eyes cast down, his fingers drumming on the table. Interestingly, I never had a moment's doubt that I would get the chance to work with him. After all, this was Israel, was it not? I was there, he was there, everything was beginning, so why not?

Kaplan told me to come the next week to the tree nursery station at Gilat, on the way to Beer Sheva, to begin work. "It is a trial, you understand? Only a trial!" For me, it was permanent. As had happened to me before and would happen again in the future, I went for it fully, as if it were the most obvious development in my life.

8

The Tree Nursery Station at Gilat

I arrived at Gilat a week later, in mid-November 1954, during the kind of rainstorm that happens only in semi-arid places. Not the soft and continuous rain of the northern countries, which is so much a part of those green landscapes and the rhythm of life. Here it poured against the land. The heavens had opened in water, a new deluge, to finish the earth once and for all. I descended from the bus and stood there, soaking wet within minutes, and unable to discern anything in front of me.

When I crossed the hundred or so yards to the office of the tree nursery, I found there two men and a woman. They looked incredulously at this person who had emerged through the water curtain. No, Kaplan had not come. The implication was that no sane person would come in such weather. The four of us sat around the office, staring sadly out at the rain. Later I came to share the feelings, typical of reforestation people, evoked by such a deluge: so much water, so much needed, so wrongly distributed, what a loss, what a loss. . . . We sat there for a long time; nobody seemed able to move.

Forty years later that part of the Negev is one of the most pleasing landscapes in Israel. Soft hills under a blue sky, much green, intensive agriculture, pretty *moshavim* (cooperative villages) here and there, a general feeling of modest prosperity. In 1954 it was all still patchy: new immigrants from all the ends of the earth had been hurled together, in hastily built little houses. They were supposed to make a living in occupations they did not know, in an unfamiliar climate and in the framework of a cooperative village structure imposed on them from above. Gilat the tree nursery station was on one side of the road, Gilat the *moshav* was on the other side. Since I shopped at the modest grocery store in the moshav, I came to know some of the people there. The village looked anything but hopeful. As a newcomer myself, I understood the bewilderment of the inhabitants. Nevertheless, with the experienced eyes of a former youth movement activist, I saw here and there youngsters who already looked different. The Hebrew they spoke had a different inflection. They were probably pupils at the nearby agricultural school. They already moved around as if they owned the land. And indeed they did.

Compared to the village, the tree nursery station was attractive. It included a low building for the administrative offices, some small houses for the permanent staff—two drivers, the administrator, the mechanic/plumber—and their families. The station was enhanced by what was then probably the best gardening and landscaping in the Negev. Nearby were fields with the tree nurseries.

I lived in a room with the administrative clerk, an immigrant from Iraq who had already completed his military service, where he had learned Hebrew. I surprised him by bringing to the room what for me was, after a bed, the most essential piece of furniture: a little desk I had found in some corner.

My professional initiation into forestry started from the bottom: loading trucks with boxes of samplings that were distributed for planting all over the northern Negev. From time to time I rode in the trucks and participated in the planting, and this became my favorite job. My salary was very modest, but so were my needs.

The human environment at the tree nursery was extremely interesting. The work with the tree samplings was delicate and was generally done by women, who belonged to two main groups. One group comprised Iraqi women who lived in Beer

Sheva (about ten miles south) and were brought every morning by truck. The other group was made up of Yemenite women who came from Bitha, a nearby *moshav*. The Iraqis were mostly young girls. The Yemenites were of diverse ages, some girls, many married women. There was also a group of men who did the heavier tasks at the tree nursery, or went out to plant trees or care for them. Some of these men came from Yemenite Bitha, and some were Kurds from Patish, another *moshav* not far away. Some came from Gilat, on the other side of the road. The women dictated the rules of behavior at the tree nursery.

Each ethnic group kept to itself, mostly at work, always at lunch. The Yemenites were an impressive lot. While the Iraqi women, the two Yemenite men and the younger girls had all assumed common Israeli working clothes, the married Yemenite women wore traditional garb: long embroidered dresses, under which dark narrow pants descended to the shoes. The dresses had long sleeves, and thus the women were entirely covered. They were all dark-skinned, frugal, thin but strong. They came from a semi-rural environment in Yemen, and were used to land work. I was told that their village, Bitha, was one of the few in the region that was doing well. The Yemenite and Iraqi workers were all still very fresh immigrants: Arabic was spoken more often than Hebrew. Even my inexperienced ears detected significant differences in the Arabic spoken by each group. And it took some time before I was able to understand their heavily accented Hebrew.

In the whole tree nursery, I was the only "European" Jew working in the fields. I was something of a curiosity, although I did not understand this: my usual good insight into social situations had still not adapted to the new reality. My condition also gave me an advantage: I was accepted, to some degree, by all the different groups. It was an enlightening experience. Gradually my eyes opened to the human characteristics of those immigrants from Muslim countries. The Iraqi and Yemenite men and women were extremely friendly and courteous. Occasionally, however, their openness would be disconcertingly blunt. The Yemenite women went directly to the point: Why did I not marry? Why not with this or that girl (a Yemenite one, of course)? The girl in question was usually sitting in the group, listening unashamedly as her qualities, child-bearing and related ones, were explicitly described. It was all part of a ritual. There was much gesticulation and much laughing, but it was all very serious. I soon learned to cope with such behavior and never to react as one would in a European setting, that is, not taking them seriously enough.

Life in Gilat was not monotonous, although I had no radio, and there was no television or movies. After a day of work I still had to look after myself. I arranged to eat one meal a day at the home of one of the drivers. A woman in the nearby *moshav* took care of my laundry. Most shopping was done in the village, but twice a week there was a car to Beer Sheva. I had two books with me: an English edition of Tolstoy's *War and Peace* and the third volume of Max Weber's *The Sociology of Religion* (in German), the one that deals with the ancient Hebrews. I was trying to improve my German reading skills, but Weber's complex style and interminable sentences were a sore trial. However, after some months I knew both books so well that I was able to return to my childhood habit of opening a book somewhere in the middle and reading as long as possible. Which was never for long. In Gilat one went to bed early and rose at dawn.

To the extent that I ever became an Israeli (something I am not entirely sure about), the process began in Gilat. I became used to the landscape and the climate. Summer came quickly in the Negev; there was practically no spring. By March it was already hot. Because I am light-skinned, I have always had to take care not to get sunburned. My stay in Gilat was the only time in my life my skin got really dark. By summer I could work the whole day without a shirt. I saw Kaplan, the KKL agronomist, on his weekly visits to Gilat. My impression was that he was terribly busy. He was interested to know if I was surviving. I was. More, I was thriving. Early one evening I had a very strange experience, when I went to the moshav to do some shopping after work. On the way back I was suddenly overcome by such a feeling of happiness that I stood as thunderstruck in the middle of the road. "If only time would stop now, forever," I prayed.

ᘐ

One day in early February when Kaplan was visiting Gilat, he called me into the office. Would I like to work as his assistant and be responsible for some experimental forestry work he was doing, or planning to do, in different parts of the Negev? I jumped at the chance.

Now my work became extremely interesting. In the morning I would go off with a group of workers to some chosen site to plant new tree species. We would return again for watering (each parcel received a different quantity of water) and for observation, and all our activities had to be carefully recorded.

Dealing with the workers was an experience in itself. The first thing they did was take my measure as a "boss:" to find out if I was a *tembel* (a jerk), or if I was "serious." They were obviously hoping for a jerk. Work assignments were carefully defined: a specific number of trees to be planted, or tree-holes prepared. But the workers would try to dig more holes—shallower than required—so as to earn more. There were rivalries between diverse groups of workers that had to be controlled. It was best to make up a work crew with men of the same ethnic origin, but this rarely happened.

One day I was sent to the Green Forest, near kibbutz Urim, not far from what was then the Egyptian border. We were to excavate canals along the tree lines, at the rate of twenty meters of canal per day. Workers who managed to accomplish more were paid accordingly. I had two groups of workers from nearby moshavim: one made up of Moroccan Jews and the other of Kurds, Jews from the Kurdistan mountains. The Kurds were an impressive group. Dark, well built, with long beards, they had worked the land in their native country. The Moroccans usually managed to complete the day's assignment; some of them even did a bit more. By contrast, there were several Kurds who each excavated forty meters!

The next day we set to work to continue the excavations. In mid-morning, however, a border incident occurred nearby, and the Egyptian army began to shell kibbutz Urim from across the border. Here we stood in the middle of nowhere, twenty workers with only two guns! We took cover in the excavations, hoping the army would come and evacuate us. While we waited, I opened a conversation with the Kurds. They told me about the troubles they had in their *moshav*. The settlement was composed of Jews from Tunisia and from Kurdistan. The Tunisians, who had arrived first, had taken all the plum jobs—the administrative positions, the grocery, the garage—and they were treating the Kurds like second-class underlings. One of the Kurds had even been beaten up. "But why don't you react in kind?" I asked, having seen how strong they were. "Oh, no," said one of the forty-meter excavators, obviously a leader of the group, "we don't do that. We are Jews!"

❧

July and August came. During the hot summer no tree-planting could be done. I had settled well into Gilat, but now I began to worry about my Hebrew. I still did not read the language well, and I was even worse at writing it. Since work was slack and would not begin seriously again before winter, it seemed to me my time would be better spent studying Hebrew somewhere. The best notion seemed to be to take a course for several months in Jerusalem. I spoke about it with Kaplan, and he agreed. I would come back for the winter season. It was only a temporary break.

9

Jerusalem

Ulpan Etzion, a well-known institution in Jerusalem, specialized in teaching Hebrew to adults. Thousands of
immigrants passed through Ulpan Etzion during their early days
in Israel, later becoming active citizens in all the professional
sectors of their new homeland. For students who had nowhere
to stay, the Ulpan also offered living quarters and a restaurant.
The class I was admitted into was made up of people like me:
mostly in their twenties, already Hebrew-speaking, but wanting
to attain a higher level. The teachers had a great deal of experience in their field, and some truly saw their task as a mission.

Unfortunately, I was far from being an ideal pupil. I have
always been a poor student of languages, in spite of the fact
that I know several of them. Also, I disliked the atmosphere at
the Ulpan. Most of the pupils were new to the country, and
there was a general feeling of dissatisfaction and insecurity.
This malaise was expressed in sharp criticism of the "establishment," against this or that characteristic of the school, of Israeli
life or life in general. In addition to the constant complaining,

my fellow students frequently exhibited a deep pessimism and suffered bouts of depression.

Their negativism bored me. I was on a different track, optimistic, curious, opening myself to the new environment, beginning to know the country. I took a room in the neighborhood and avoided involvement in the social life of the Ulpan. In the afternoons and evenings I took long walks through the city. Here, obviously, was something highly interesting for me: Jerusalem. I literally sniffed the city. I took in her peculiar colors, paid attention to her peculiar human types. This was the beginning of an affair with Jerusalem that would continue forever. But after two months at Ulpan Etzion I became impatient. It was September, and there were still about two months remaining until my return to Gilat. One of the students at the Ulpan was going to study at the Hebrew University, and he suggested that I audit some classes. This made sense to me: through reading Weber's *Sociology of Religion,* I had become very interested in the history of the biblical period.

I went to see the academic secretary of the university, Abraham Carmel, to ask for permission to audit some Bible classes. "Had I finished high school?" asked Carmel. "Could I bring some certificate?" Well, it was a touchy question. As youth movement leaders, we had not cared about school certificates. We had already graduated, so we believed, from an upper echelon academy of life experience, and with flying colors. Formally, I had finished (barely) that technical school for construction, which in Brazil would have allowed me (perhaps, depending on my grades) to try to enter an engineering school. But a background in humanities, and in Israel? With only a scanty knowledge of Hebrew? I decided not to pursue the matter; in any case I would have been able to participate in classes for only a short period.

About a month later, an uncle of mine in Tel Aviv became ill. I went to see him, and while I was there I visited the Brazilian embassy, to ask what could be done about my precarious school record. The woman at the embassy took what I would describe as a pragmatic view of my inquiry. What did I need the certificate for? For studies at the Hebrew University? "Of course, no doubt—here, take this letter certifying that you are entitled to it." The letter was adorned with a huge seal at the bottom.

As it was now October, classes at the Hebrew University had already started. Although I had only a few weeks left before returning to Gilat, I went again to see Abraham Carmel. There was a long queue. When my turn came, the over-worked academic secretary apparently no longer remembered who I was and what I wanted. He read the certificate, contemplated the impressive seal, and looked up:

"But classes have already started!" He was right, what could I say?

"Yes. . ." I mumbled. Carmel sighed deeply. Life was such a mess. . . .

"All right, all right. . . . We accept you . . . . Here, take these forms, fill them out, leave them with my secretary. Shalom, shalom. . . . The next one, please."

At that moment I grasped that a huge blunder had been made. The academic secretary had forgotten, or perhaps had misunderstood, about the auditing for which I was seeking permission. He had accepted me as a regular student! Although it had never occurred to me to do so, at that moment, not a second before, I decided to enroll as a student at the Hebrew University.

∾

The next two months were a period of unmitigated confusion. I had not the slightest idea about how to organize my program of studies. I had no money. I must look for a new room. I returned briefly to Bror Hail. My sister Ruth, who had recently arrived there from Brazil, was keeping my few belongings. I packed some things and went back to Jerusalem. I arrived there on a hot morning, typical weather for Jerusalem in October, the last days of a *hamsim*. I faced the question of where to live. I looked at the city like some conqueror of old, considered hills and valleys, views and distances, and chose a spot: there.

"There" was a hill in Abu Tor, above St. Andrew's Hospice, not far from the railway station, fifty yards from what was then the Jordanian frontier. An old, two-story house stood at the top of the hill. I noticed a terrace on the upper floor. I went up the hill, into the house, up to the second floor. Dogs barked. A man carefully opened the door and held it barely ajar. He was not suspicious, but he was surrounded by dogs and cats, which he wanted to keep inside.

"I am a student. I just came from the kibbutz. Do you have a room to rent?" By evening I had rented the most beautiful room I have ever had. Huge with walls one-yard thick, and filled with light from three windows. The adjoining terrace I had seen earlier faced the walls of the Old City, Yafo Gate and the old Mishkenot

Shaananim quarter. It was within walking distance of the Terra Sancta building, where the Hebrew University had its provisional location after losing the Mount Scopus campus in the 1948 war.

Arye, the owner of the flat, was a Romanian who had survived the war in Europe. After the war he made a fortune in the black market, in the Russian-occupied zone. Before leaving Europe he converted everything into gold, but the Russians caught him trying to cross the frontier and searched him, and he lost all the gold. Now he lived in the three-room flat with four dogs and two cats. Between one deal and another he studied jurisprudence, and later he became quite wealthy again.

In the late afternoon I could hear from my room the *muezzin*, the Muslim crier in the Old City, calling the faithful for evening prayers. At the very same time Arye would open his window and call out, in a powerful voice that rolled over the valley: "Pierre, oh Pierre, where are you? Pierre!!!" Pierre was not some new and competing deity, but a huge tomcat, who soon appeared faithfully for his dinner.

Downstairs from us lived a couple, Sabina and Eli Schweid, who invited me to share their Shabbat dinner. Eli, then a graduate student at the Hebrew University, later became one of Israel's outstanding intellectual figures. During our first dinner together, he and I quarreled over the structure of Tolstoy's *War and Peace*, to Sabina's chagrin. A lifelong friendship had begun.

The next question was how to support myself. I had papers from Brazil proving that I had worked as a professional journalist, and I was able to get a job as translator and editor for Portuguese at the Jewish Agency. The work was on a piecemeal basis, which was convenient for a student. But the arrangement was too shaky: sometimes there was money, sometimes not. Later I began preparing radio programs in Portuguese at the Israel Broadcasting Authority. And thus another problem was solved.

In the middle of all this I went to see Kaplan, in the same office in Jerusalem where we had met the first time. Less than a year had passed since my last visit, but it seemed like a decade. I told him that I would not return to Gilat for the winter. I would study in Jerusalem, and go back after finishing. Kaplan listened in silence, looking at me with his large, soft eyes. He understood the situation much better than I did. This was Israel, was it not?

Everything was beginning, everybody moved. It was part of the rhythm of things.

I had not yet fully grasped how much my life would change. After I finished my B.A. in 1958, I went back to Gilat, to consider what to do about my career in reforestation. I soon found out that my heart was no longer in it. After two weeks I returned to Jerusalem and went to see my tutor, Shmuel Ettinger.

"Shmuel, I have decided to come back. I want to continue my studies."

Ettinger, another wise man, looked at me with an expression of mild surprise:

"I never thought you would not!"

Nothing is more difficult than to know oneself, and it rarely happens in time.

10

Studies at the Hebrew University

I was already twenty-five when I started my studies at the Hebrew University in the fall of 1955. This was my first experience of a university and academic lectures. I remember my B.A. studies as a kind of protracted intellectual feast, to which I came with a strong hunger. I took classes in every subject, from sociology to Jewish mysticism. The more I heard, the more curious I became.

Only years later did I learn something about the inner workings of that peculiar institution, the Hebrew University. All I knew then were the famous names of some of the teachers, and I went to hear them with great expectation. I took a class with the great Jewish historian, Itzhak Baer. His appearance was unforgettable. Many years later, in the Bodemuseum in East Berlin, I saw a fifteenth-century wooden statue of a Christian saint that was an uncanny reminder of Baer: tall, gaunt, a long and bony face, his mind attuned to some inner world. I could not understand him in class. My Hebrew was still limited, and Baer spoke the language in the heaviest German accent I have ever heard, delivering his lecture staccato fashion. There was a total lack of contact between him and his students. He was immensely courteous yet also immensely distant. Baer addressed students in the third person: "Has he read that article?" It was necessary to answer him the same formal way—a very unsettling situation for loose-mannered young Israelis.

A different experience was listening to Gershom Sholem. In one of the last courses he gave before his retirement, he was explaining Moses Cordovero, the important sixteenth-century kabbalist who had a relatively "rationalist" orientation. Sholem was a lecturer, not a speaker. The analysis was sober and intellectual. There certainly was nothing theatrical in Sholem's presentation. Nevertheless, he created a spellbinding, almost hypnotic atmosphere. Somehow his lectures, as if reflecting his field, had an intensely non-rational quality.

A student enrolled at the Hebrew University was required to study a set of themes from the perspective of two different disciplines or two different departments; he was also required to do a confusing array of general studies. A friend helped me organize my study plan, focusing on the Bible Department and the Department for Jewish History, where I concentrated on the biblical period. I soon found out that I lacked the necessary preparation for Bible studies and that they did not interest me much. At my friend's suggestion I switched my course of study—two months having already passed—to general history. A year later I once again altered the direction of my Jewish history studies, from the biblical period to a concentration in modern Jewish history.

My schooling in Brazil had been disastrous. Whatever education I had was the result of autodidactic reading. The studies I undertook at the Hebrew University were my first exposure to organized learning. Sometimes the deficiencies of my former education weighed heavily. But when I found a teacher who was also a good pedagogue, it was such a pleasure to learn!

One such case was Joshua Prawer, who taught medieval European history. Prawer's lectures were uniquely lucid. The high points of the theme were precisely accentuated, the summing-up of ideas clear and logical. Prawer's level of teaching set an example for me which I tried to imitate later, when I myself became a university teacher.

There were situations, however, where my deficient formal schooling made it very difficult for me to properly appreciate a distinguished scholar. This was the case with Shlomo Pines, who was giving a course on Jewish philosophy in the Middle Ages. I went to his class. A middle-height, chubby gentleman entered, with a vague look on his face, as if he were not sure he had found the right room. He stood before us, and without using any notes he began to talk, eyes on the ceiling, holding his crumpled hat in his hand like a handkerchief. When the hour ended he stopped in mid-sentence and left. I had the impression that no one in the class had the vaguest idea what he had been talking about—at least, that was true for me.

A week later Pines returned and started anew, again without notes, again the vague look, although this time without the hat. Probably he had forgotten it in some library. The students became restless, and when he mentioned some obscure fourteenth-century Arab philosopher whose name nobody caught, he was interrupted: "What? What was the name?" Pines sighed as if awakening from some dream, looked at us, looked at the blackboard, wrote the name of the philosopher on it, turned around to face us again, and droned on—with his body obscuring the name he had written! The hour over, he again stopped in mid-sentence and left. I rushed to the blackboard to copy the name. It was written—how else?—in Arabic. I gave up and left the course.

Only later did I learn that Pines's course was put together like a cathedral: harmonious and balanced, each idea in the right place, each lecture continuing exactly from where he had stopped the week before. And all this without any notes. I simply was not well educated enough for Pines's class.

With the changes I kept making in my program, and with the additional courses I was auditing on all possible and impossible themes, my course of studies became a rather eclectic affair. But my time was relatively free.

The Israel Broadcasting Authority paid me well for my part-time position. I prepared one weekly program in Portuguese, which was taped and sent express to several Jewish radio stations in Brazil. Usually, it would arrive in four to six days. I hardly ever went to the Broadcasting Authority offices. Working at home, I would collect from the daily newspaper items that might interest my Brazilian audiences. On Saturday evenings I would spend two hours writing a news segment, add some music and prepare a commentary on some topic. On Sunday evenings I went to the studio and put it all together on tape, which would be mailed to Brazil the next morning.

Felicitous as the arrangement was, it demonstrated a significant lesson. This was my first experience with bureaucracy on a public service level. Had I insisted, the Broadcasting Authority would have provided me with a room, or at least a desk, with, of course, telephone, typewriter, and soon, a secretary. With incoming and outgoing correspondence. With meetings, consultations, conferences. These activities would mean I could no longer manage without supporting help for broadcasting, music preparation and technical services. Yet here I was doing those programs in a couple of hours, on a level no one ever complained about, and with practically the whole week free for my studies.

However, other distractions sometimes took me away from them. The second year at the university had barely begun when war with Egypt erupted in October 1956. I had not yet developed that fine feeling for political and military tensions that older Israelis have, and the onset of hostilities caught me completely by surprise. Most of the students I knew were called to their units on the eve of the war, or had already disappeared before, but I had not noticed. I had already left the kibbutz, but my military documents were still being processed somewhere between Bror Hail and Jerusalem. I went to the military command in Jerusalem to present myself for service. The sergeant-major in charge told me that without the documents he could not accept me.

"But I want to serve! There is a war going on!"

The sergeant-major seemed very tired. He probably had not slept for several days. He looked up at me, a reflective expression in his eyes, as if he were trying to understand some mysterious riddle. After a long moment he spoke:

"Tell me, are you still standing in front of me?"

No, I was not. I had disappeared.

I discovered that intercity buses were running, and two hours later I was in Bror Hail. Nobody there asked about documents, and I got a uniform and a gun. That night I kept watch. No one slept. Throughout the night Israeli armor rumbled along the main road, full lights blazing through the darkness, southwards, in the direction of the Gaza Strip.

The next morning those of us at Bror Hail were incorporated into a battalion and sent to the Gaza Strip, too. Parachute units had broken through the lines of the Egyptian army and continued on without stopping, so as not to allow the enemy to regroup its forces. They raced on until they were close to the Suez

Canal. We were sent as a second wave, to overcome any remaining pockets of resistance.

From Bror Hail to the Gaza Strip was no more than half an hour by truck. We crossed the border into what seemed to be another world, especially for me, who had never been among Arabs. Villages, houses, fields, vegetation—everything looked different. Military cars burned along the road, mostly Egyptian, some ours. We searched villages and buildings, but found neither soldiers nor civilians.

In the afternoon we received orders to occupy the village of Djebelia, where there was a huge refugee camp. At the entrance to the village, dominating the road, the Egyptians had built a large defense position atop a hill. On the top of the hill were anti-aircraft guns that had been swiveled down to point at the road where we were. Our orders were to occupy the position. I remember to this day the feeling of fear, the big black guns aimed directly at us. My companions told me later that they had felt the same. Never in our lives did we run up a hill so quickly. When we arrived at the top, we found the position completely deserted.

Night fell. A new military unit arrived, took over temporarily and then moved on. From the distance we could hear gunfire. It was dark. No food arrived, so we ate some Egyptian preserves we had found. We were exhausted. Some comrades and I fell asleep in a building near the hilltop post. When we woke the next morning, we discovered that we had slept in an ammunition depot, filled with mines, grenades and explosives. We left almost as quickly as we had run up that hill, the day before.

After several days I returned to the kibbutz. On the way back I smelled for the first time in my life that sickly sweet odor of rotting corpses. The smell was all around, although no dead were to be seen.

Three days later I returned to Jerusalem. But it took at least another week to focus attention on my life there. This delayed reaction to normal surroundings is a truism of wartime service. Later, especially after the Yom Kippur War in 1973, I sympathized completely with those students of mine who had left the war behind them, and yet who sat in class, day after day, looking at the walls, unable to find themselves truly returned.

☙

Only in my third year at the university did I begin to find a concrete direction in my studies. My interest began to focus on history, on modern history, on modern Jewish history. Although the decision was my own and had little to do with the teachers I met at the Hebrew University, the intellectual caliber of those scholars continued to astonish me. Never before had I known people of such intellect. Some professors I encountered in the Department of History—not to be confused with the Department of Jewish History—such as Joshua Prawer and Joshua Arieli, certainly influenced my own intellectual development. Yet I became most interested in the field of Jewish history.

In the Department of Jewish History I had the good fortune to come under the formative influence of two great teachers: Israel Halperin and Shmuel Ettinger. Halperin was a small man, with very sharp blue eyes, a superb methodologist. I came to know him in my first M.A. year, when I participated in a seminar he taught on a new theme, the development of the Jewish press in the nineteenth century. That seminar was a notable one: of approximately ten participants, eight became university professors.

Halperin suggested that I work on the reaction of the European Jewish press to the 1848 revolution, a theme both interesting and complex, with little background literature. I had to prepare a paper and give a lecture in class. It was my first academic research, and I went for it with true appetite, especially because I sensed that my potential was being evaluated. I thoroughly researched the sources, discovered Jewish newspapers that were practically unknown, coined definitions for new terms of reference, presented hypotheses, suggested conclusions. My essay ran for about one hundred pages. Halperin read it and told me that he would comment on it during my lecture in class.

My first surprise was discovering that it would be an "open" lecture: no time limit was specified (and it was to go on for four or five two-hour sessions!). Questions and discussions, in which everyone could participate, were conceived on the spot. The second surprise was Halperin's didactic method: he isolated each fact I presented and each analysis I had done. He questioned the facts and tore the analyses apart. He did not bother with the larger assumptions or conclusions, but went, like the true professional he was, for the structure of the essay, for the small components upon which the larger picture was built. For me, it was a long and difficult ordeal, and this went on week after week.

At the end I got my paper back. It received the highest grade possible. Indeed, that paper later became the letter of introduction for my budding academic career. "Not bad at all. Quite promising," Halperin commented, with his sardonic half-smile. Nevertheless, I was in a state of complete intellectual demoralization. It would be a long time until I dared again to affirm, in historical matters, anything about anything. But at least I recognized what had happened to me, and I was grateful to Halperin for his rigorous treatment of my work. He had dealt with me in the only way possible, considering the too self-assured and very ignorant person I was.

This was the first step in a very beneficial process of academic development. To have worked under Israel Halperin's guidance is a privilege cherished by every one of my colleagues who experienced it. Unfortunately, Halperin died in the early 1970s, while still relatively young. He honored me by chairing my Ph.D. presentation in 1970, although he was by then seriously impaired.

Actually, the first teacher who gave me personal attention was Shmuel Ettinger, whom I had met in my last B.A. year. It was Shmuel—characteristically, everybody called him by his first name—who sent me to Halperin. Ettinger, then in his late thirties and still at the beginning of his academic career, was already something of a legendary figure. Born in Russia in 1919, he had arrived in Palestine in the 1930s. In his adolescence he had been an orthodox *hasid*, and people still remembered him praying fervently. Then he had changed, and in the 1940s joined a tiny group of political radicals, the Hebrew Communists. At the time I met him he had changed again; he was then a very liberal democrat, close to the Israeli Labor Party. Ettinger became one of the most influential figures in Israeli academic life. By the 1980s, most Israeli university teachers in his field, modern Jewish history, were his former students, and had been significantly influenced by him.

Ettinger was a fascinating man, and I fell very much under his spell. His was a sparkling intelligence that found its way in fields of human knowledge that never failed to astonish my colleagues and me. He had impeccable taste: in art, in behavior, in ideas. He was a born educator. One time I met him on campus, and out of the blue he launched into an explanation of the intricacies of Rousseau's theory of the social contract and the problems regarding personal liberty this theory provoked. His remarks left me reflecting for a week.

As historians, Ettinger and Halperin were opposite types. Ettinger wrote little, and with great difficulty, but was a very good speaker. Halperin wrote a most elegant Hebrew, but was terrible as a lecturer. As an historian, Halperin was a superb craftsman. Ettinger never bothered with the ropes of the profession, although he knew them exceedingly well, He went for the idea, the principle, the historical process. It was the privilege of many people of my academic generation to have studied under both men. We respected Halperin very much, but we loved Shmuel.

Ettinger was a highly controversial man, extremely subjective, and certainly apt to change his opinion. His advice was sometimes of unique value, but it could also happen that he was completely wrong. With Shmuel it was always a matter of extremes. The result was that many loved him, some hated him, but no one remained neutral. Later our ways parted. However, it is impossible to deny the deep influence he exerted on me and my work.

The third of my academic mentors was Haim Beinart, with whom I developed a close friendship. We became acquainted toward the end of my M.A. studies. Beinart's career had been far from easy. Although he had developed into an international authority on medieval Spanish Jewry, it was claimed by some that his academic work was too "technical," not "imaginative" enough. Indeed, Beinart worked more in the German academic tradition: restrained, very professional, and with unique mastery of the sources. Beinart was one of the smartest men I have known, with a faultless sense of judgment about people. In all the years I knew him I never saw him fail in human evaluation. More than once I had to recognize, sometimes years later, that in our diverging opinions about a give person Beinart's judgment had been wiser than mine.

Beinart was decisively helpful at three major moments in my academic life. In 1965 he became the dean of the Faculty for Social and Humanistic Sciences of a new institute for higher learning then being created in Beer Sheva; this institute became Ben Gurion University. He invited me there to teach modern Jewish history. It was my first teaching position at the university level. In 1976 he secured me an appointment at the Hebrew University that opened the way for my later integration there. Then, one morning in 1979, I got a phone call from him:

"Evyatar, I am here at the Carta Publishing House, and there is this project . . . hmmm, could you come over, so that we can talk about it?" Carta was nearby, and when I got there I found Beinart with the publisher, Emanuel Hausman.

"Evyatar, would it interest you to prepare an atlas on modern Jewish history?" Now, my historical work had been in the ideological and political direction. About geography, demography, statistics and atlases I had not the slightest idea. That may explain how I accepted the proposal on the spot—besides the fact that I had learned to trust Beinart. I did not know it, but I had embarked on one of the most interesting, albeit most complex, intellectual adventures of my life. I look at that atlas today and am overwhelmed that I managed to do it. Had I known what its compilation would involve, I would never have accepted the offer. Which once again proves the advantage of innocence over experience.

11

First Academic Steps

Until I began my M.A. studies, I had not thought about an academic career. In the early 1960s, between the end of my M.A. studies and the beginning of my Ph.D. dissertation work, I had two opportunities to deepen my involvement in Jewish history. I became a research assistant at the Weizmann Archives, where a large authoritative edition of the Weizmann papers was being prepared—a task that would take years. And I secured a second part-time position, again as researcher, at the newly established Institute for the Research of Zionism at the University of Tel Aviv. Both jobs were related to academic topics in which I was interested. Weizmann was the theme of my Ph.D. thesis and the Weizmann Archives the principal source of material on the Zionist leader. At the University of Tel Aviv I was able to continue the research on American Jewish history which I had begun in my M.A. thesis.

At the Weizmann Papers enterprise I worked under the direction of two very competent scholars, first Me'ir Vereté and later Gedalya Yogev. Vereté was a remarkable man. His field of specialization was nineteenth-century English foreign policy. He had an awesome reputation as a scholar: high intelligence and an excellent memory, and he insisted that everyone express himself, orally as well as in writing, with care and precision. Vereté had an interest in historical detail and a store of knowledge that continually surprised his colleagues. In addition, he was endowed with a fine historical instinct that, in conversation, would express itself in unexpected questions. His inquiries always went straight to the marrow of the issue.

Vereté was, however, a very difficult man to be or work with. He was sarcastic and demanding, although never rude. But he loved to indulge in nasty comments about his colleagues, the more well-known the colleague the nastier the observations.

"Yesterday I saw Yankele Talmon [Jacob Talmon, of *The Origins of Totalitarian Democracy* fame]," he would tell me (and everybody else) with great satisfaction. "I asked him: 'Jacob, have you read Leonard Stein's new book, *The Balfour Declaration?*' 'Yes,' Talmon said to me, 'I examined it *(iyanti bo)*'. 'No, Jacob, what you want to say is, you skimmed through it *(difdafta bo)*!' " Such stories, and similar ones, did not exactly make Vereté the most endearing man in the academic community.

I owe to Vereté a very important lesson in that most complex field, intellectual morality. Without being aware of it, many scholars I have known are less than inquisitive intellectually, less than rigorous when it comes to the evaluation of ideas. It does not mean that they are corruptible: they would never accept an idea if asked or paid to do so—even under pressure. But many of them are quite defenseless against that most subtle weakness, which imposes itself from the inside: they are unable, or worse, unwilling to ask the hard questions, to reevaluate the established preconceptions of their social, intellectual or spiritual environment. I came to understand, helped by Vereté's example, that established values are exactly the ones a scholar should, if not doubt, at least examine carefully, critically. That kind of questioning is the scholar's most basic duty, the moral content of his or her intellectual calling. Inquisitiveness does not protect a scholar from error, and to question does not mean that established concepts and values cannot be accepted—far from it. But to fail to do so certainly constitutes a sin against one of the major moral commandments of a scholar.

That lesson was driven home to me in 1967, on the fiftieth anniversary of the Balfour Declaration. Vereté had been invited to give a radio lecture on the Declaration. Now, in Israeli political folklore, the Balfour Declaration has, or had then, a mythic quality. It was seen as some meta-historical agreement between Great Britain and the Jewish People. In a low-key tone, completely unemotional and with copious use of documents, Vereté went on the radio and demolished the myth. From a British point of view, he said, the Balfour Declaration was an expression of British political interest, political interest only. The Zionists, the Zionists had been manipulated ever so subtly by the British, whose aim was to achieve full power in Palestine through them—although they had managed it as if they, the British, were only responding to the Zionists' wishes. Or, as Vereté stated it at the end of an article he published later, with his typically dry humor: "To my mind it calls the story of the lady who—as the saying goes—was willing, and only wanted to be seduced. Britain likewise willed Palestine, wanted the Zionists and courted them. Weizmann happened to come her way, talked her to have the Zionists and go with them to Palestine, as only her they desired and to her they would be faithful. Britain was seduced. She was ready to be seduced by any Zionist of stature."

The radio lecture, and the subsequent article, caused a public and academic scandal. I remember a "private" discussion among university people in Ettinger's house, with about twenty scholars and some graduate students present. Vereté explained his point of view. After ten minutes everyone was shouting; only Vereté remained calm. He could not have cared less about the whole commotion. I, myself, sat in a corner, objectively unconvinced by Vereté's case, but subjectively aware that I was witnessing an instance of intellectual conduct that I should consider very carefully.

To say that Vereté was incorruptible would be an inadequate description: he simply was beyond such things. I recall one instance that illustrates my point well. For obvious reasons, the identity of one's Ph.D. judges is one of the most carefully guarded secrets at the Hebrew University. In 1970, shortly after I delivered my Ph.D. dissertation to the university, I got a phone call from Vereté:

"Evyatar, I was nominated as judge of your dissertation." My heart missed a beat. To have Vereté as judge was the nightmare of all my colleagues. And to learn of it in such a matter-of-fact way was unheard of. "Evyatar, would you please bring me your files of documents, so that I can check your sources?" I literally felt my heart sink into my stomach.

"But Me'ir, most of the documents I used are on microfilm. I have a card collection with the microfilms attached, but there are thousands of pages of it!"

"Hmmm, and how do you read them?"

"I have at home a small microfilm reader."

"Excellent, Evyatar. Please bring me the reader and the card collection."

I hauled everything to his room at the university. He worked on it for a long time. One of the things I take special pride in is the fact that I "passed" with Vereté as my Ph.D. judge. I never discovered who the other judges were. Nor did I care.

As a person—not as a scholar—Gedalya Yogev was carved out of softer wood. He replaced Vereté as chief editor of the Weizmann papers—Vereté was too uncompromising a personality for the editorial board. Gedalya was patient and discreet, hated controversies, always looked for compromise and understanding. As historian he was a first-class professional, the best historical editor I have ever worked with. He died too early, but the twenty-three volumes of the annotated edition of the Weizmann letters are a dignified memorial to him. Even if he did not live to prepare them all, he built the framework for the whole edition and established the criteria and level of research. I did not work long with Yogev at the Weizmann Archives, but we remained on close terms and were to meet again later on.

My professional connection with the Institute for the Research of Zionism at Tel Aviv University did not last long either. In 1966 Israel suffered an economic recession. Jobs were cut, and I was fired, the first and—so far—only time this has happened to me. However, in the long run my ties with the institute proved extremely positive and congenial. The scientific relationship was maintained, and the institute was prepared to publish two of my books, both in Hebrew: *The Zionist Movement in the United States, 1898–1914* (1970), and *The Political Development of the Zionist Movement, 1917–1922* (1977). Furthermore, many of my research essays were published in various journals of the institute.

In retrospect, I consider myself lucky that my first academic work was related to research. I was allowed to spend time acquiring knowledge and working toward what would become articles and books, while many of my colleagues were mired in time-consuming and poorly paid jobs as teaching assistants.

In the 1960s I developed whatever professional skills I possess as historian. During this decade I spent most of my time in archives, in Israel and abroad, searching for and collecting documents, and developing a system that would allow me to use my sources efficiently. I learned that it would take as much time to organize documents properly as it would to search for them. And that both tasks taken together, searching for and organizing the sources, would be more time-consuming than the subsequent writing. I discovered also that, at least in the humanities, there is no general system for organizing one's historical sources. Everyone has to determine, through trial and error, the way of work best adapted to his or her type of mind.

Furthermore, I learned that many decisions about professional tools or directions of work that seemed quite objective were strongly influenced by subjective leanings. A typical example is the decision about which path to follow among the diverse historical schools: intellectual history, social history, etc. One's teachers play a role, as do the ideological influences of the learning environment. But it is most important to understand one's personal turn of mind. Each person of average intelligence may be able to work successfully in an uncongenial field. However, truly creative work can only be accomplished in a field one has the touch for.

One's work is also influenced by trends and fashions, which occur in academic professions as anywhere else. For instance, in the 1960s and 1970s, everybody became very keen on oral history. Since my themes of research dealt with the twentieth century and there were participants in my historical happenings who were still alive, I was supposed to interview them all. I did dozens of such interviews, and almost always the results were disappointing. One essential rule of oral history (which most interviewers do not comply with) is that one must know more about the theme dealt with than does the individual being interviewed. Even then, one will, as a rule, only get some information about peripheral details. Considering the time and money consumed by the institutes for oral history that were created during that period, I could not fail to question the discrepancy between the cost involved and the limited results obtained.

Sometimes, indeed, I met notable people in the course of these projects. One effort in oral history that rendered no concrete results, but was unforgettable in itself, was a conversation I had with David Ben Gurion in the late 1960s. Ben Gurion was by then in his eighties and lived in Sde Boker, a kibbutz in the central Negev. A student of mine, Zeev Tsahor, had worked as his secretary, helping Ben Gurion with his memoirs, and he arranged the contact. Back in 1920 Ben Gurion had participated in the London Zionist Conference. I needed to know more about that gathering, one of the most troublesome in Zionist history, and documentation was notoriously sparse.

Sde Boker was about an hour south of Beer Sheva, in the desert. Ben Gurion lived alone in a little house, attended by some bodyguards who doubled as housekeepers and also prepared his very modest meals. Inside, the house gave an impression of comfortable simplicity; it had about three rooms, each one filed with books. In spite of his age Ben Gurion appeared fit, and looked as I had imagined him: small, compact, the famous aureole of white hair. He behaved in a simple, direct way. The spark of the man, the famous Ben Gurion temper that had kept a whole generation of Israelis on their toes, was no longer there. But a reflection of it remained in his eyes: they were small and mean. Ben Gurion's eyes were the meanest I have ever seen.

He remembered the London Conference, but only in a very personal way. His wife Paula was sitting in the gallery during his speech, with their little daughter on her lap, and the child had cried. I learned nothing further from him about the conference.

On two other occasions, however, I got results. These were not exactly "oral" history, since in neither case did I actually meet the person I contacted. The first of these occurred in the late 1960s. While finishing my book on the Zionist movement in the United States, I found out that Joseph Jasin, who had been the secretary of the Federation of American Zionists in 1910, was still alive. We corresponded. He had an excellent memory and quite a number of past scores to settle. I was able to check his information with other sources and confirm the accounts he gave me. But it was in the second case, with Julius Simon, that I struck gold.

Before World War I, Simon had belonged to the second echelon of the German Zionist leadership. Since he also had American citizenship and was close to Chaim Weizmann, he was called to London several months after the Balfour Declaration, to take charge of the Zionist office being built up there. For a short and tempestuous period during 1920 he became one of the central figures in the Zionist administration. Then he committed a not uncommon political mistake. Simon admired both Chaim Weizmann and Louis D. Brandeis, the two most prominent figures on the Zionist scene in 1920. During the so-called "Brandeis-Weizmann struggle" that shocked the Zionist movement in 1920–21, Simon tried to maintain a working relationship with both sides—but like several others he ended up being crushed between the two factions. In the spring of 1921 he resigned his position as executive secretary of the London Zionist Office and later emigrated to the United States.

That period, 1920 to 1921, was a crucial focus of my Ph.D. dissertation. I think it was Ben Halpern who told me that Julius Simon was still alive and living in Princeton, and suggested that I write to him. Simon answered in a very neat longhand that betrayed no sign of his eighty-eight years. His mind was still sharp as a razor, and his blood still boiling over what had happened almost fifty years before. He was happy to have found somebody with whom he could go over it again. He was still furious with himself, almost fifty years later, for relinquishing his post. At that time his position was one of great influence in the Zionist movement. Giving it up had obviously been the greatest mistake of his life. "Never resign!" was the message he kept repeating.

I never met Julius Simon, but we corresponded for four years, until he died—not of old age, but of cancer. He had an incredible memory: I once sent him some obscure minutes of a crucial meeting—between Brandeis, Weizmann and supporters of both sides—that had taken place in London in August 1919. Simon was able to elucidate and correct the garbled version. He was categorical: "I remember that meeting word for word!" The changes he suggested in the text of the minutes were corroborated by other evidence. Suddenly, the text made sense. I was completely convinced.

Simon's remembrances went back to the beginning of the century. He had been in Palestine before World War I. Once, on a visit to *kvutza* Degania in the Jordan Valley, he had made the acquaintance of the grand old man of ethical Socialist-Zionism, Aharon David Gordon. After the war, in 1919 or 1920, they met again, this time in Europe. "Have you learned Hebrew yet?" Gordon had asked. Simon, who had not, made an apologetic movement with his hands. "You know, I am so terribly busy, and my head. . . . " "No," Gordon answered, "the problem is not your head, it is your heart."

Simon had written his memoirs, which he sent to me. When I came to the United States in 1970, he was already dead. I visited his widow, Ellen Simon, in Princeton, and we settled the details about a book on Julius that would contain the edited memoirs, letters, an essay and other pertinent material. At the end of my visit Ellen arranged for me to meet Simon's last secretary, a very proper middle-aged lady. We went out for coffee, and she talked with me about Julius, how much she had enjoyed working with him, how much Simon had enjoyed our correspondence— especially when he succeeded in proving that I was wrong on this or that point. At the end, we took our leave of each other at the bus station—I was on my way to the airport, back to Israel. I saw that she hesitated. Obviously, there was something she still wanted to tell me. Finally, it came out:

"You know why it was such a pleasure to work with Julius? Because he was a ladies' man!" And she left.

Julius Simon—Certain Days, Zionist Memoirs and Papers, my second book, appeared in 1971.

12

Living in Jerusalem

In 1960 I married. My wife, Batya, was a student too. We were lucky to find a comfortable old house in the Bak'ah neighborhood, built of solid stone, which we later managed to buy and gradually renew. Our three children were born there: Noa in 1963, Hillel in 1966, Ofra in 1969. In 1962 my parents settled in Israel, too. The growth of my family, my studies, the beginnings of academic work, all came together with the experience of living in Jerusalem, that strangest of all cities.

When I arrived there in 1955, Jerusalem was divided between Israel and Jordan. There was virtually no contact between the two parts of the city. The borderline which criss-crossed the city was as ugly as any urban boundary and dangerous as well. There were frequent incidents, and several times I was forced to lie down on the street, because shots were being fired from the Jordanian side of the line. Older inhabitants explained to me that it was impossible to recognize the city in her present condition. Indeed, after 1967, when Jerusalem was reunited, I understood what they meant. Suddenly the city took on a completely different atmosphere. Dividing Jerusalem was like tearing a complex masterpiece in the middle.

While I was living in Jerusalem I went through my second war in Israel, the Six Day War, in June 1967. At that time I was serving in an auxiliary unit. Although fully mobilized, we actually saw very little action. But the battle for Jerusalem was hard and bloody. During the night from the ninth to the tenth of June no one slept. Fighting raged in the Old City. The big roof of the Dormition Church on Mount Zion burned like a huge torch, illuminating the town. Jerusalem was reunited, but it was through no peaceful deed.

Some weeks later the borders between the two sectors were opened. I was working in my home at about nine o'clock in the morning when a very excited Arab gentleman burst through the fence shouting: "peace! peace!" Overcome with emotion, he embraced me. He told us that he owned a pharmacy on the Arab side of the partition. Years ago he had lived in our house, or perhaps it was the house of our neighbors, and now he was able to return. His happiness was contagious. We exchanged greetings, addresses, good wishes. Alas. . . .

In the afternoon my family and I went to visit the other part of Jerusalem. It caught us like magic. From then on we went back each afternoon, for weeks and weeks; we never had enough. But I came to understand what the oldtimers had been saying about the trauma they had experienced with the division of the city.

Perhaps it is the atmosphere of Jerusalem. Perhaps I had been conditioned in advance. But from the moment I first arrived, I was aware not only of the city's peculiar charm, but also of a certain challenge she embodies. Jerusalem is a place that invites one to walk. One has to do it by day, by night, again and again, to get the full sense of her. It takes time. The first impressions I sorted out were relative to the apparent contradiction between the tumult of Jerusalem (the city is in danger of being strangled by traffic), her multifold tensions, and the serenity that in certain hours seems to envelope the city like a cloud. Not only does Jerusalem have more than one personality—many cities do. The unique feature is the character of her diverse faces. There is the human dimension of the city, and there is Jerusalem as such: she has a living quality of her own. I have known two places where the human presence is something like a tolerated oversight: the Sinai Desert and Jerusalem. It is as if the city's inhabitants, with their petty interests and silly quarrels, are but an accident: people come, people go. They have been coming and going for centuries—believers in many creeds, preachers of many truths—and Jerusalem has seen it all.

Jerusalem leaves no one indifferent. Indeed there are some who find her extremely oppressive. I had a friend from Tel Aviv who occasionally came up for business, but left as soon as it was accomplished: "I cannot stand that city, with all that stone! It challenges you, it forces you to define yourself!" Indeed, Jerusalem demands that one take a stand, declare one's attitudes. Every issue, every question, appears to acquire in Jerusalem a seriousness, a disturbing inevitability. My friend was right: there is no easy living in Jerusalem. But it suits me well enough.

However, life in Jerusalem can be complicated. I have known few other places where a person can be as lonely as in Jerusalem. It has to do with the fact that people there do not live in broad "society," but in small groups, where relations are in-bred, stable, even defensive against an outsider. The idea that Jerusalem can be defined as a city of three different religions is an inexact generalization. In fact, each religious group is divided into many subgroups, according to ethnic origin or religious shading, and each one lives within its own walls. To penetrate into one of the social groupings of the city is far from easy. Worse, once you get into one, it is strangely difficult to get out.

My own natural group, when I settled in Jerusalem, would have been that of new immigrants, from South or North America, many of them students at the university. I avoided those people from the start. I wanted to become part of "older" Israeli society. My closest friend during my student years, Joseph Shatzmiller, who later became a distinguished scholar and professor of medieval history, was a typical Israeli. Batya, my wife, was an Israeli, and the home we established was of course Hebrew-speaking. As much as one can become part of something by choice, I became a Jerusalemite. But then, was it not the same with so many others who had come? With all the obstacles that Jerusalem puts in the way of newcomers, if one manages to find one's place, there is nothing superficial about the integration into the city.

Teddy Kollek, the eminent mayor of Jerusalem for almost thirty years, once said that the population of Jerusalem is a mosaic, not a melting-pot: diverse human groups live there, and have been living there forever, side by side, but not together.

However, they have learned to know one another, and influenced each other in subtle ways. For instance, although people know that in religious matters I am non-observant, no one ever telephones me on *shabbat*, nor would I call others: one does not do this in Jerusalem. Everyone takes care not to hurt the feelings of one's religious neighbor. One is much more tolerant regarding the religious way of life—though not regarding religious politics—than people in other cities. The tolerance is all the more notable, since it generally operates only in one direction: from the secular side toward the religious sector. The great majority of Orthodox Jews live completely isolated in their own neighborhoods. I often ponder the irony of the declarations of Orthodox politicians when certain religious issues are discussed: "To change this (or to accept that) will split the Jewish people into two separate parts!" In fact, we are split. An Orthodox Jew would never eat in my home: it is not kosher, or not kosher enough. Our children rarely meet: they live in separate quarters, they study in separate schools. All my children went into the army; daughters of Orthodox families do not, and in the case of extremely religious Jews, neither do the sons. Is it possible for us to be separated further?

Another thought-provoking experience is the everyday encounter with Arabs. Actually, only after 1967, with the reunification of Jerusalem, did we meet Arabs in daily contact. Reality, one learned then, had little to do with existing stereotypes. The Arab painter, the shopkeeper, the car mechanic, are people like us, and it was in the nature of life that we came to know each other, and to develop good relations with some. In normal times, it was possible for Jews and Arabs in Jerusalem to coexist exceedingly well. I never forgot this, not even later in the 1980s, when relations between the two groups became very difficult. Beyond the normal daily contact, one could easily get lost in the fog of political fantasy and public hysterics, as easily on the Jewish as on the Arab side.

Living in Jerusalem has decisively influenced my own process of "israelization." In fact, I wonder what exactly an Israeli is. I see myself rather as a Jerusalemite, a Jerusalemite academician. That is also the way, to my mild surprise, I am seen by others. One time I met a prospective donor to the Hebrew University who was staying at a hotel on the Tel Aviv seashore. After we finished our talk, I left and went back to Jerusalem. The weather was hot and humid. I stopped a cab, whose driver was fat and sweaty. He seemed rude. ("Those Telavivis. . .", I thought). He took one look at me and asked: "From Jerusalem?" On the way to the bus station we talked. After two minutes I was aware that I had been caught in a stereotypical prejudice against Telavivians: far from being rude, the man was courteous and thoughtful.

Those differences between Jerusalem and Tel Aviv are a theme for endless jokes ("To Jerusalem one goes on pilgrimage; to Tel Aviv, on expedition. . ."). However, there are some distinctions; Israel has gradually formed diverse human types. Considering the small dimensions of the country, this seems strange. Yet it is not: one of the surprises of Israel is that in half an hour one can travel between different geographical conditions. From the mountains of Jerusalem to the Dead Sea, twelve hundred feet below sea-level—another climate, another landscape, another world—takes only thirty-five minutes by car. Between Jerusalem and Tel Aviv, less than an hour apart, there is the additional difference of the social environment. Telavivians seem to dress and behave in other ways; they have their own mentality. Life in Jerusalem is quieter (but not calmer, and certainly more perplexing), and it is affected by those two human influences, Orthodox Jews and Arabs, which have much less impact on Telavivians.

&

There have been times when I despaired of Jerusalem, its tensions, its quarrels. One gets tired of all the fanatics and lunatics that the city seems forever to breed or to attract. Some are wild-eyed, but some—the worst—are all sweetness. We had one Christian neighbor, a short American fellow, a very nice person. Once I asked him what had brought him to Jerusalem. "Well, isn't it the right place to be? After all, the end of the world is near, isn't it?" And if it wasn't the end of the world, it was the imminent arrival of the Messiah. I learned that it was better not to ask.

And then there are those special hours which compensate for everything. I can happen on a certain afternoon in winter, when suddenly the color of the city turns violet. Or early on a summer morning, when the sun literally bathes Jerusalem in light. There are clear days when one can see every detail of the mountains of Moab, on the other side of the Jordan Valley, sixty miles away. One stands breathless at the sight of Jerusalem like a splendid woman dressed for a grand gala.

Mostly I love Jerusalem, although sometimes I hate her. One may occasionally feel like a tolerated incident in the centuries-old identity of Jerusalem, but one is caught by her. Jerusalem is a burden, but a burden one carries, sometimes with pride, sometimes with humility. I wish I had been born in Jerusalem. I am happy that my three children were.

13

Ben Gurion University

At its creation, the Negev Institute for Higher Education was a small affair, an office and some classrooms in the HIAS guest house in Beer Sheva. The idea, however, was to develop a multifaceted university, with faculties for the humanities, social sciences, engineering, natural sciences, medicine and veterinary studies. Several Israeli universities had agreed to participate in its academic development. Courses were to start in October 1965. In September, Chaim Beinart, obviously in consultation with Ettinger, offered me a chance to teach modern Jewish history there. It was my first teaching appointment, and I took up my post three weeks later.

Most of the faculty members came from Jerusalem. Many of us were Ph.D. students with no previous teaching experience. Some had teaching positions in Jerusalem and took on the appointment in Beer Sheva as a second job. After 1967, when the road through Hebron opened, we travelled from Jerusalem to Beer Sheva in little more than one hour. We would arrive in the morning and return in the evening; sometimes we stayed overnight if there were meetings or if we had classes two days in a row.

Everything considered, the development of Ben Gurion University of the Negev, as it was named in 1972, happened very quickly. In the early 1970s we moved to the new campus. Academic structures, rules and programs were decided upon, a very comprehensive program of studies was established, and academic departments and faculties were functioning. Yet the university lacked the kind of experience that comes with time, that personal and intellectual stability which is so vital an element in an university. People came up with ideas and plans that might or might not be sound. Soon the faces changed, new people appeared with new plans. The only way was to live through it, and be as careful as possible.

In the meantime, I was doing quite well in Beer Sheva. There was much interest in academic studies in Beer Sheva and in the surrounding small towns and villages, and we had plenty of good students. I enjoyed teaching. After the first year came a second, and a third. Before long we had students who were finishing their B.A. Soon we were teaching a full program, covering all four historical periods: biblical times, the Second Temple-Mishna-Talmud period, the Middle Ages and the modern era. In 1968 I became responsible for the Department of Jewish History, and two years later I was formally named chairman. There were about twelve teachers in our department, most of them young, and some began to move to Beer Sheva. We were the first in our faculty to organize a proper department and employ teaching assistants. Soon we had B.A. students continuing their work on M.A. degrees at the Hebrew University, and eventually M.A. studies were established in Beer Sheva.

The growth of the Department of Jewish History was much facilitated by the excellent relations I enjoyed with the dean, Chaim Beinart. Rarely have I worked so well with anybody. We respected each other's opinions, so we were able to cover a whole agenda of issues in about thirty minutes. I also developed a very good working relationship with the first rector of Ben Gurion University, Haim Hanani. Soon I was participating in further academic tasks. In addition to teaching and heading the department, I became chairman of the university's library committee, and a member of other important faculty committees.

Although I do not remember it that way, 1969 must have been the busiest year of my life. My wife, who had finished her studies in clinical psychology, was working toward a psychoanalytic career. We were in a situation typical of so many young Israeli families, trying to manage our lives between professional training and obligations, young children, low incomes. Besides all the tasks at Ben Gurion University, I was busy with the galleys of my first book, on American Zionism (which was to appear in 1970). I was also finishing my Ph.D. dissertation, collecting material for a book on Julius Simon, and preparing several articles.

One distraction I hated, but learned to live with, was the military service, which took up one month every year. Because I had back problems, I had been transferred to an auxiliary unit, so I did my service, mostly guard duty, in Jerusalem. I did this year in, year out, for twenty-five years. The army seemed to have a knack for calling me at the wrong time: when I had reached a crucial stage in an article or had an urgent lecture to prepare. Since there were long stretches of free time during the service hours, I always carried along a briefcase with work: galleys for my next book or some essay in preparation. I particularly remember working out some central ideas of a chapter in my book on the Zionist movement in the United States in 1967, while I was mobilized during the Six Day War.

Obviously, there were some tension-filled hours, but I do not remember being overworked or short of time. It is incredible how much one is able to accomplish when things go well. When I finished my period as chairman of the department in 1973 and my friend and close collaborator Baruch Eyal was elected instead, I felt quite satisfied with what we had accomplished. However, we were to learn that success breeds as many headaches as the lack of it, and perhaps even more.

One problem that soon emerged reflected the instability of a still young university. Less than a year after Baruch Eyal became department head, we read in the newspaper—nobody had bothered to tell us about it—that a well-known Israeli professor of established seniority, whose field was Jewish history and who had been living in the United States, had accepted a position in the Ben Gurion University and was to become our "colleague" in the next academic year. This was the first appointment that had not been decided by us. Worse, it had been made without consulting us. In addition, it was an appointment that, for several reasons, we would never have made ourselves. It struck us like a very cold shower. By then other circumstances at the university had changed as well. Beinart had finished his period as dean and was back in Jerusalem. Hanani was no longer rector. Obviously, the new rector had decided to teach us a lesson about the realities of life: we were a bunch of assistant professors who had done a good job—indeed, so good that it was now time to call in a real pro. Several months later our new colleague arrived. My first private conversation with him confirmed my worst fears. The man was a prima donna. He would never fit into the kind of working relationship that had developed among the teachers in the department.

As became clear afterward, the university had made a grievous mistake. Troubles that had nothing to do with us soon arose between the professor in question and the academic heads of the university. About a year later he resigned and left. But the feeling of assurance and accomplishment we had felt in our department had been deeply damaged. Indeed, we were still only assistant professors, and without the protective umbrella of a Beinart and the sympathetic eye of a Hanani, it was doubtful that we could hold our own in the tough arena of a developing university.

Furthermore, I had a personal problem brewing. My successful work at the university brought pressure on me to move to Beer Sheva. The university's policy called for the academic staff to live there, so as to "participate in the life" of the university and of the town. I was sympathetic to the point but disliked the principle: my life and my family's life were nobody's business but our own. In addition, as much as I enjoyed Ben Gurion University, its atmosphere and its rough openness, I disliked the town of Beer Sheva. As happens with most cities created by fiat from above, Beer Sheva had not yet evolved its own character. The place was hot and barren, and I found it very ugly. It was hopeless to compare it with Jerusalem. I argued that my participation in the life of the university was fuller than that of many people who lived in Beer Sheva. This was, however, a self-defeating argument: if I lived in Beer Sheva, the administration rebutted, I would participate even more.

In addition, the hiring of the unsuitable colleague described above sharpened certain doubts I had about the direction and the priorities of Ben Gurion University. From the beginning, the emphasis at Ben Gurion had been on engineering and the natural sciences. Was the university intended to become an institute for technological sciences, with a handful of humanities studies annexed as a kind of decoration? Or would it develop in such a way that all the fields of higher learning were emphasized equally?

I had several extremely frank conversations about this issue with leading colleagues from other departments. I argued that the humanities give a university its individual character. In theory it might be possible to establish an university with only a faculty of humanities. But while an institution whose main emphasis is on natural sciences and engineering might become a good institution for higher technology, it would never become a university.

My interlocutors agreed, and yet I remained doubtful. The more I spoke with them, the more I wondered what they actually made of my arguments. Some of the physicists and chemists I knew were extremely smart and very positive people, but we thought differently, our methods and minds were directed toward diverse goals. Those of us in the humanities thrived on questions; the answers did not matter that much. The scientists were geared toward answers. This essential disparity led to divergent attitudes toward the university, its organization and its goals.

Theory apart, there were new realities at Ben Gurion University. The natural sciences and engineering developed much faster than the humanities. Academic advancement, too, is usually faster in those fields. Among the engineers, the physicists, the mathematicians, it is not unusual to find full professors who are in their forties, even their thirties. This is not true in the humanities, especially if the tradition of the Hebrew University— where advancement comes notoriously late—is influential in an institution. The result of such a situation was most evident in the leading councils of the university, where crucial decisions about how to cut the financial cake were made. At this level there was a whole battery of heavy guns from the exact sciences, extremely clearheaded about what they are after— money—and a few scrawny cats from the humanities, defensive and torn by metaphysical doubts about right and wrong in higher education.

I began to question my future at Ben Gurion University. I was scheduled to go to the United States on sabbatical in 1975, and I decided to postpone my decision until my return. However, while we were away, something happened that decided the issue for me. In my absence the dean, in collusion with one of the teachers in our department, staged a mini-coup: they

merged the Department of Jewish History with the Department
of (general) History, something I strongly opposed and would
have done my best to avert, had I been around. Which of course
they knew.

At first glance, there seemed little justification for the tradition of two separate departments, but this was the arrangement
that had first developed in the Hebrew University and had been
adopted later by other Israeli universities. Did not historians in
both fields work with similar methodologies? Were not Jewish
historians supposed to have a thorough training in general history? Would not the interaction between scholars from the two
fields benefit everybody? In addition, the chronological span
covered by our department seemed too long: from biblical times
until our own day. Academically and methodologically speaking, it was argued, there was greater affinity and mutual interest
between a scholar working on nineteenth-century German history and one who was interested in the Jewish history of the
same period, than between someone who specialized in the ancient Hebrew kings and a colleague researching the evolution of
American Jewry in the twentieth century.

However, the structure of the Department of Jewish History
was neither arbitrary nor thoughtless. It was built upon that
most legitimate (although not always stable) fundament, a concept: that the Jews had been a people from biblical times until
the present, and that the ultimate aim of the study of Jewish
history was to understand, in spite of current scientific specialization, the underlying ideas and dynamics historically tying that
people together throughout the centuries of its existence. If indeed the Jews had been a people, the same people, from biblical
times until the present day, it was important for historical research to explain what that unique "peoplehood" meant.

There was a second consideration. Undoubtedly, there were
excellent historians in the Department of (general) History. However, English, German and several other histories were well covered in many European and American universities, where large
numbers of scholars were employed and did impressive work.
Jewish history, we felt, must be brought to the highest possible
level in Israel, for it had much less chance of development anywhere else. Research on Jewish history in an Israeli university
was permeated with its own peculiar, particular tension; here it
could be extremely creative, and it should be allowed to flourish

without being forced into other academic frameworks. These considerations justified the separate existence of a Department of Jewish History, although it should be in close contact with similar disciplines in other academic departments.

Unfortunately these considerations meant nothing to the new dean, an American more impetuous than reflective, and with little knowledge of Jewish studies. Nothing made more sense to him than to unify the two historical departments and establish the biblical period, together with archeology, as an independent department. Was this not the way it was done in American universities?

The dean was probably an adept of the idea that the best defense is a strong offense. When I returned from my sabbatical year and discovered that "my" department had disappeared, he avoided discussing the reorganization with me, deciding instead to force the issue of my residence. Either I would move to Beer Sheva, I was told, or. . . . For all the reasons mentioned, work at Ben Gurion University had lost its appeal for me, and I decided to quit. The fact that no one really tried to convince me otherwise only showed that I had already lost the battle.

Looking at the way matters developed after that, I have no reason to alter the opinions I had then. Ben Gurion University developed mainly in the direction of the natural sciences, medicine, and engineering. The academic leadership remained concentrated in the hands of professors who were active in those fields, but whose understanding of the humanities was limited. The decision about the departmental reorganization was clearly a mistake. As a result, a young and promising department of Jewish history was, for all intents and purposes, abolished. To my knowledge, even the new unit dealing with the biblical period never developed properly. The rigid policy regarding residence in Beer Sheva had the inevitable disadvantages of rigid policies in general. A much wiser attitude, although a more difficult one, would have been to be flexible on that matter. Allowing a non-academic issue to become holy principle meant that local settlement, instead of academic quality, became a central criterion for academic employment. Those who taught at Ben Gurion University might not always be those most qualified to do so, but rather those who were ready to live in Beer Sheva. The academic quality of the faculty was hardly improved by the university's residential policy.

14

Brazil, Twenty Years Later

In the middle of the Beer Sheva period of my professional life, during the summer of 1974, I returned to Brazil. More than twenty years had passed since I left the country where I spent my adolescence. I had been invited by the Department of History at the University of São Paulo to teach a course on modern Jewish history. The invitation was initiated by an old friend, Nachman Falbel. Falbel and I had first met in the youth movement, in São Paulo, and had become very close. Later he had come to Israel and lived for about ten years in Bror Hail. Nachman had left the kibbutz, studied history at the Hebrew University, and later returned to São Paulo and developed into a very respected scholar of medieval church history. Besides the academic assignment I was offered, which I considered important, I was extremely keen to see him again.

My life had undergone major changes in the two decades since I was last in Brazil. I had left as an aspiring pioneer, to join a kibbutz in Israel, where I intended to specialize in some branch of agriculture. I returned as a university lecturer in a wholly different field, modern Jewish history. In the intervening years, I had submerged myself in a new culture (my third): first as a student on the fringe of society, gradually as a full participant. I had studied Jewish history and the many facets of Judaism with famous scholars and teachers; I had progressed, and was now myself writing books and articles. I had participated in multifold and interesting academic activities which shaped my views and my personality. I had married, and my wife and I were raising three children. We had established a home in Jerusalem. I was a full-fledged member of Israeli society.

São Paulo, the city of my youth, had changed enormously in those years. Indeed, the city was virtually unrecognizable, and I could no longer find my way around. When I left in the early 1950s, São Paulo was already the economic heart of the country, dynamic and fast-moving, with a unique atmosphere and a relatively stable population. The megalopolis I returned to was completely different. Beginning in the late 1950s, Brazil's economic expansion had been phenomenal, and much of it had been concentrated in and around São Paulo. By 1974 there must have been well over 10 million inhabitants in São Paulo—nobody knew for sure, since day after day waves of newcomers arrived from the impoverished Brazilian hinterland, attracted by illusions of a better life in that new Eldorado.

São Paulo had literally been erased and rebuilt from mid-1950 to mid-1970, with new streets cut through the city or erected over it. Yet the city had grown much faster than all the urban plans, which by themselves seemed much too drastic. The result was very confusing. On the one hand, there was Avenida Paulista, whose opulence reminded one of New York's Avenue of the Americas. On the other hand, the city was encircled by huge neighborhoods of African—no, worse, Brazilian—poverty. São Paulo had also become a city with an intolerable level of dirt, noise, and pollution. I remember standing on a street corner, waiting for a taxi and about to smoke a cigarette. The air was so heavy with fumes and odors that I suddenly felt I would suffocate if I lit that cigarette. I threw it away: it was the last cigarette I ever smoked.

The poverty was heart-breaking. It was impossible to ignore the utter misery that gnawed at the tails of so much opulence, the squalor one met everywhere in Brazil, the terrible level of criminality that was one of the consequences of so much deprivation in the shadow of so much richness. Crime was considered "natural," inevitable, like the rain and the sun. I was assaulted twice, in the middle of the day, in the very center of the city, with hundreds of people around me; one assault took place just outside one of the most expensive hotels in town. None of my friends dared to walk around wearing anything valuable; a thin gold chain around the neck was dangerous, for one might literally be strangled if the chain did not give way when pulled. Yet it was considered prudent to carry some "rescue money" to give to a potential assailant so as to avoid his wrath and knife.

Why did people stay there, I asked myself. For most of acquaintances of my youth, Brazil had truly become their home, even if they had not been born there. In addition, most of then had begun in modest circumstances and prospered; indeed, quite a number of them were becoming very rich. This did not make them more likable. Their houses were ostentatious, cluttered with tasteless yet expensive bric-a-brac. They lived barricaded behind the walls of well-defended residences, moving around in closed cars and developing a jungle-defense mentality. São Paulo had become an uncontrollable megalopolis. Rapid modernization had produced both new fortunes and utter poverty. Social structures were in disarray. I had long talks about this with Nachmann Falbel, one of the few who had resisted the "trends." He shared my stupefaction.

Yet I realized that a very significant component of my sense of alienation from São Paulo and from Brazil had less to do with the country's transformation than with the changes that had taken place in myself. Talking with friends from the past, I was able to reestablish contact, at least on the surface, to relate experiences, bridge the distance of two decades. On a deeper level, however, I felt I was a complete stranger. Had my former integration into Brazilian life been less profound than I had thought? While this was a possibility, I wondered. Strangest of all (and I experienced this again, when later I returned to Germany) was the fact that my unaccented Portuguese and my familiarity with Brazilian manners and customs heightened that sense of foreignness and alienation. I felt as if I had landed on another planet.

I was mature enough to recognize the situation I found myself in and analyze its components. More, I tried to break the circle of isolation in which I found myself and to recreate contact with the local environment. I feasted again on native food, always a good indicator of cultural integration. I tried again the dishes I had loved as a boy. *Feijoada*, the Brazilian national plate, made of black beans, rice and meat, with *farofa* added, was as delicious as ever. I drank again *caldo de cana*, sugarcane juice, which as a boy I used as a test to establish who among my immigrant friends had become "Brazilianized": those who did not like *caldo de cana* still had a long way to go. I devoured *empanadas, doce de coco, goiabada*, salads of delicate hearts-of-palm. I tried again the food of Bahia—that astonishing cuisine—a refinement of slave cooking expressed in a wide variety of dishes. As a culinary experience, it was delicious, and I went through it all with my stomach almost unharmed.

I read new authors and reread the older ones. The great classics, like Gilberto Freire's *Casa Grande e Senzala*, that superb sociological description of the nineteenth-century *latifundia* of northeast Brazil, where slaves and senhores met and mixed in strange and peculiar ways. I enjoyed again *Os Sertões* by Euclides da Cunha, his beautiful account of the rebellion of the *jagunços* (cowboys) led by Antonio Conselheiro in the early twentieth century. I pored over the literature of my adolescence: Machado de Assis, Érico Verissimo, Jorge Amado, the poetry of Castro Alves, and many others. I even reread the classics of Portuguese literature, to reacquire the full feeling of the language, and I became once again enamoured of Eça de Queiroz and his uniquely powerful and flexible language.

I went to see once more the painters who had taken my breath away in my youth, such as the powerful Cândido Portinari and the great Lazar Segall, half-Jewish immigrant, half-Brazilian. I listened to contemporary Brazilian music. I had always liked Villa-Lôbos, one of the first truly Brazilian classical composers, who had broken away from the Italian-dominated tradition and done for Brazilian music what Grieg had done for Norwegian or Albéniz for Spanish music. In the 1960s and 1970s there had been a rich flowering of popular Brazilian music of a very high level. I loved the honest sentimentality of Vinícius de Morais and became fascinated with the talent of Sérgio Buarque de Hollanda: his song "Construção" seems to me one of the most moving and sophisticated pieces of popular-classic culture I have ever heard in any language.

I revisited the places of my childhood and adolescence. Beautiful rua Paissandú in Rio de Janeiro, lined with high palm trees, where we had lived in 1939 after arriving in Brazil. As a child I had contemplated, at the end of the street, the impressive Palácio Guanabara, which had then been the official mansion of

President Vargas. Some streets away, near Praça do Machado, I found the Liceu Franco-Brasileiro, the first school I attended after arriving in Brazil. I went there in the afternoon, and the school was already empty, but the porter let me in. The classrooms, the tree-lined patio, the blue-painted walls, everything looked surprisingly as it had thirty-five years before—even the large soccer-field, where I discovered as a boy, to my lasting chagrin, that I was not good at all in that game I had come to love.

Yet the more I tried to reestablish contact with Brazilians and Brazilian culture, the more alienated I felt. I could not understand what was happening, and toward the end of my stay I became quite anxious. When I left Brazil, after finishing the course at the University of São Paulo, I firmly intended never to return again.

Subsequent circumstances brought me back to Brazil several times, usually in connection with some professional activity. At such times I would again visit the familiar places of my younger years, and if it was still a bittersweet experience, it was less painful than it had been during that visit in 1974. Gradually I came to terms with my peculiar foreignness. Each visit to Brazil became easier. Since I expected less, I was able to find more. I was able to disconnect myself for several weeks from my other worlds, and I immersed myself in the rhythm of Brazilian life, more aware this time of the limitations of my situation. Gradually I arrived at a new understanding of Brazil, the country and its life. I came to see Brazilians and their behavior in a new light.

I began to grasp more fully some of the factors that hold Brazilian society together, in spite of the social injustice and the shocking juxtaposition of ostentatious riches and appalling poverty. I believe that one factor behind their social cohesion is the exceptional humanity that most Brazilians, of whatever social level, have in common. I came to recognize the unusual kindness of Brazilians, their cordiality, their flexibility, their readiness to make the best out of a deplorable situation. Once I gained proper perspective, I came to recognize and respect the most beautiful quality of the Brazilians: their tolerance of other people.

While living in Jerusalem I had become very much aware of the importance of tolerance. Probably no other place in the world is so cursed as Jerusalem by a wild-eyed collection of fanatics of every creed and persuasion. Tolerance as a social norm has interested me since my youth. My formal studies helped me to understand the phenomenon of tolerance in the European context, that precious and sometimes fragile flower cultivated through so many philosophies and with such hard efforts. Tolerance, proclaimed as an ideal by proponents of the eighteenth-century European enlightenment, had struggled to survive the onslaught of nineteenth-century nationalism, but then was virtually suffocated in the dark first half of the twentieth century. European tolerance, with its philosophical foundations and political aims, was the result of persistent efforts by different and quarrelling peoples who basically were not tolerant at all. Brazilian tolerance, on the other hand, is natural. Rather than being a result of the country's political system, it has strongly influenced its very structure. It certainly has roots and reasons, which are the sociologist's and historian's delight. Whatever the explanation, it is there. And it certainly is one of the central elements keeping Brazilian society together.

In the end, my later Brazilian experiences brought me to a few significant insights, some personal, some of a more general meaning. One is that each person is bound to live, for better or worse, in the present and not in the past. For a historian, ever asking himself about the significance of past events, it is no simple matter to reach such a conclusion. Today I believe that while our past may help us to understand our present, even enrich it, its influence on our present has limits we should understand as clearly as possible.

The second insight represented, in spite of its ambiguity, the other side of the same coin—in fact, I grasped it first, although logically it comes second. Gradually it dawned on me that the searching, more than the finding, had led me to return, again and again, to those places I had known in my younger days. For there was nothing to find in Brazil (or later, in Germany) but memories. Memories, the selective impressions left by past events ever so carefully filtered through the obscure meshes of our mind, fulfilling an equally obscure, albeit essential, role upon our self-awareness. Memories, those phantoms who had begun to pass occasionally through my consciousness. Memory cannot, should not, acquire too strong a hold over our present concerns. But what can we make of our present-day life if remembrance is not there, adding sense and color to the background of the scene on which we move and act? The searching was an effort, more than merely to know, to "perceive" myself better. It was a trip in and of the soul, a very personal, very solitary inner voyage, mostly sweet and gratifying, sometimes harsh, even scary, but always infinitely important.

15

Teaching at the Hebrew University

      In 1977 I began to teach full-time at the Hebrew University. This was no easy period for me. In Beer Sheva I had been one of the founding fathers of the faculty and eventually acquired a personal status that left me relatively untouched by petty university tensions and quarrels. By contrast, in Jerusalem I was only one teacher among others, many of them fiercely competing with their colleagues on matters relevant and (mostly) irrelevant. My professional position at the Hebrew University was still undefined. The fact that relations with my former tutor, Shmuel Ettinger, had begun to cool did not help either. At Ben Gurion University I would soon have attained a full professorship. In Jerusalem it would take many long and unnerving years.

      In Beer Sheva I had been fairly judged on the basis of my academic qualifications. In Jerusalem my academic deficiencies were emphasized. True, my early intellectual upbringing left much to be desired. Between emigrating and immigrating, I never acquired what may be called a primary language. I dared to teach in several languages, but in none could I publish without significant editing. My Hebrew never attained the high level that was expected in our department, and my immersion in Jewish culture remained inadequate. No matter how long I studied, I could never compare with a Jew or an Israeli who had had a good Jewish education from childhood, especially one who had also studied in a *yeshiva*. My rather abrasive personality (others would perhaps describe it in harsher terms) did not help either. What advantages did I bring to my new position? I enjoyed work, had some good ideas and a certain amount of common sense. And, when all is considered, I had a lot of luck.

The cooling of relations with Ettinger gave me much to think about. We never quarrelled openly—Ettinger was too much of a gentleman for that—but we hardly spoke. For someone who owed him as much as I did, this required a measure of adjustment. My own explanation of the situation is that deep down we were antagonistic personalities. One way of viewing Ettinger was to see him as a hasidic rebbe, although one molded into a modern frame. He kept around him a court of adepts and admirers, who worked with him, or on themes he was interested in, or adopted his approach to historical issues. Among those disciples one could discern all the jealousies, and all the tensions, of a hasidic court.

That hasidic dimension, I feel, is one of the reasons I was wary of Ettinger. Now, I, too, am of hasidic stock: my father's family had been connected with the Rishiner Rebbe. They once lived in the Ukraine, but moved to Galicia on the instructions of the rebbe. My father had in him many hasidic characteristics and ways of behavior, and I see them in myself as well. However, I am a rebellious *hasid*. I hate hasidic courts, and the delicate play and underplay of influences and counter-influences that go on there.

Nor could I stand the style of work that went on in Ettinger's court. It was too much like a debating society, where the emphasis was on discussions, lectures, conferences, commissions, rather than on the kind of hard-core historical research I first learned by working with Israel Halperin. My research areas were outside Ettinger's interests and expertise. I focused on American Jewish history, Zionist political history, German Jewry. I would disappear for weeks or months, immersed in my work like one possessed. I was unaware of what was happening around me—nor did I care. "Were have you been?" Shmuel would ask surprised, when I surfaced again. "Working . . ." I would reply. I would reappear with a new article, some chapters of my Ph.D. dissertation, the outline of a book.

Ettinger was apt to be inconsistent, and on one occasion his inconsistency led me to break with him permanently. Even though he was my Ph.D. instructor (my dissertation focused on Chaim Weizmann's Zionist activities after World War I), he took little interest in my extended research, insisting instead that I follow a certain line of thought. There was in Zionism, he claimed, a specific position of ideological character which in some way was related with and to Weizmann, and deserved to be called "Weizmannism." It was an intriguing point. Weizmann was a statesman with an eye for the feasible and the practical, more than for ideological direction and consistency. However, Shmuel had an excellent historical instinct, and something in his thesis made sense: there seemed to be a leading idea that had not only inspired Weizmann, but had also been developed by him, although he had no objective perception of doing so. I reflected on this issue for some time, and established what I came to define as the outline of "Weizmannism." Indeed, this outline became the ideological backbone of my dissertation, which I finished in 1970 and which earned Ettinger's praise. Incidentally, Weizmannism as an ideological or semi-ideological line of thought is accepted today by most historians of Zionism, even if there are differences regarding its precise framework.

When I returned to Israel in 1976 from the United States, after my first sabbatical, I was invited to give a public lecture at the Israel Historical Society. Since Ettinger was one of the leading figures of the society, what theme could I choose for my lecture that would be more appropriate than "Chaim Weizmann and the Development of 'Weizmannism' "? I prepared a well-reasoned presentation. When it was over, Ettinger got up and criticized my lecture at length. He insisted that there was no such thing as "Weizmannism." I was dumbfounded. I literally could not believe my ears. After that we continued to maintain correct, sometimes even good relations. However, it had become clear to me that I must find my own way in university circles, without Ettinger's help.

This was not easy. Personal ties are relatively important in academic life. It is one of the results of academic inbreeding, a system very common at the Hebrew University: faculty members are usually chosen from among the most gifted graduate students in each department. There are many different responses to academic inbreeding. In the United States it is severely frowned upon. At the Hebrew University it is an unwritten rule, and has been adopted by most other Israeli universities.

At the beginning, I thought I could see the merits of the system. It allowed the development of an academic tradition, especially in relatively young institutions. The lack of academic tradition was one of the greatest weaknesses I had observed at Ben Gurion University. More recently, however, I have become quite critical of academic inbreeding. It is apt to stultify independent thinking. If one rubbed the wrong side of one of the reigning professors, one's career might be jeopardized. It also produces something like an old-boys' network, giving preference to familiar colleagues rather than superior candidates, when new appointments are to be made.

Sometimes inbreeding expresses itself in funny ways. Shmuel Ettinger frequently quoted one of his teachers on a particular issue. Later on, when I referred to the same issue, I quoted Ettinger, quoting his mentor. Recently I learned that one of my former students, who is now a professor at an Israeli university, explained the same point in these words: "As my teacher, Professor Friesel, used to say in the name of his teacher, Professor Ettinger, in the name of his teacher, Professor Roth. . . ." The style, at least, was Talmudic.

My integration into the Hebrew University's Department of Jewish History was not, then, an easy process. However, I had time to research and write, and I was in a good position to ponder that very complex institution, the Hebrew University of Jerusalem. A description of this institution could be drawn from a cultural, historical, or even sociological point of view. But beyond these considerations, the university is excellent material for literature, as writers great and not so great have already discovered.

Judging by the number of its students—about 16,000 in the 1970s—the Hebrew University was not especially large. But size did not matter; there were very distinguished academic institutions in Europe that were much smaller. What made the Hebrew University important was its emphasis on the scientific fields that were researched, taught and excelled in. I had my own experience of this expertise while preparing the atlas of modern Jewish history in the early 1980s. There was no topic for which a specialist could not be found at the university or near it for consultation. Expertise was available on patterns of

Jewish demography in certain neighborhoods in Johannesburg to internal religious divisions in German communities after the Secession Law of 1876, on the migratory patterns of sixteenth-century Sephardic Jews in Europe to demographic characteristics of nineteenth-century Yemenite Jews, and so on.

There were significant differences between various faculties, and between different departments. Those established before World War II were rooted in Central European traditions. The ones that were created in the 1950s were strongly oriented toward an American academic perspective.

The Faculty of Humanities was a central component of the Hebrew University, and at its core was the Institute for Jewish Studies—of which my department, Jewish History, was a segment. Founded in 1926, at the same time as the university itself, the Institute of Jewish Studies was youthful by European standards. In Israel, it was one of the most venerable institutions of its kind. Indeed, "old and traditional" was the first general impression an entering student of my generation had of the place. Many of the teachers who were then active were among the intellectual giants of our times. Such scholars as Gershom Sholem, Itzhak Baer, Ben Zion Dinur, Hugo Bergmann, Richard Koebner, Martin Buber and many many more were the objects of stories and legends. The famous first chancellor of the university, the controversial Judah Leib Magnes, belonged to that same group.

When I first enrolled as a student in the fall of 1955, I was able to listen to the last courses of some of the giants of that older generation. Not until much later—when I was already myself a member of the faculty—did I understand the peculiar tensions that pulsated in the faculty, the roots of the strange stories that were told and retold with gusto in Jerusalem and all over the Jewish world. As Yossi Shatzmiller once remarked: "You are like a small pond of water with very big fish inside. There simply isn't enough space for all of you to swim around." All things considered, I wondered. Of course, there were controversies, as in any university, aired in that odd way typical of many academic quarrels, where people with high intelligence clash with great intensity over matters mostly unimportant. Nevertheless, behind some of the confrontations there were real issues, which mostly remained in the background, not easily recognizable. Some very true spiritual problems of modern Jewry found poignant expression in the intellectual labors of the scholars associated with the Institute for Jewish Studies and in many of their discussions.

One had to have some knowledge of Jewish history to understand what it was all about. From a historical perspective, the institute could be seen as a culmination of the long process of cultural modernization that modern Jewry set out on during the eighteenth century. First the *Haskalah* (Jewish Enlightenment) had begun, and its labors continued throughout the nineteenth century and into the twentieth. One of its aims was to explore the roots of Jewish culture by using the scientific tools and methods of analysis that Jews were acquiring from the Gentile's world of learning. This examination, it was hoped, would bring about a new, modern understanding of historical Jewish life and to foster a continuing expression of Jewish cultural self-awareness.

The social and spiritual realities of modern Jewish life made this development a very difficult process. New Jewish culture had to compete for intellectual breathing space. It found itself placed between two high walls that, throughout the nineteenth and twentieth centuries, threatened to close in on it. On one side there was traditional Jewish religious learning, which viewed the *Haskalah* with suspicion: were these Jewish enlighteners not harbingers, God forbid, of assimilation? On the other side beckoned the great Gentile world, filled with intellectual riches, where a gifted Jewish scholar could do exceedingly well in the spiritual as well as the material sense.

Despite these constraints, Jewish enlightenment managed to carve for itself a modest niche. Jewish studies, practiced according to the methods of modern European learning, were developed by scholars mostly associated with the rabbinical institutions founded in the nineteenth century in Western Europe (and later in the United States), and by some Jewish learned societies. The scope was modest, the available means meager. There was nothing to compare with the flourishing European and American universities, where, incidentally, more and more talented Jewish intellectuals were finding a home.

The Institute of Jewish Studies of the Hebrew University deserved to be seen as the first large-scale Jewish attempt to develop a modern institution where Jewish studies would be practiced on a scale similar to that of any other university. By the time I became a student at the university in the 1950s, the effort had been spectacularly successful. The long list of departments dealing with Jewish history, language, literature and philosophy, and the numerous research institutes associated with it, had attained a position of academic leadership in the Jewish world and respect in the international community of scholars. The institute's achievements had also influenced, directly or indirectly, departments of Jewish studies in other universities created in Israel after the establishment of the state, as well as programs of Jewish studies throughout the world.

However, from a careful evaluation of the human and intellectual fabric of the Institute for Jewish Studies, one could learn something about the difficulties of the effort. All of us—my teachers, my colleagues, those of our disciples who became active in Jewish studies—continued to deal with the problem of finding the right equilibrium between the general and the Jewish components of our work. Many of my teachers had had a traditional Jewish education, including *yeshiva*. For people like me, however, more general elements in our formation had a stronger influence. One difficulty was that the very concepts of "Jewish" or "general" components were themselves generalizations. There was more than one Jewish intellectual or spiritual tradition, and there were diverse European Gentile intellectual traditions. Significant differences between the European-oriented and the American-formed faculty members further complicated the issue. All of us met somewhere in the middle, but this convergence required a continuous effort that was never easy or simple. Each solution had its personal aspect, which was likely to lead to a clash with other possible solutions to the same problem. Many of the controversies that arose among us were genuinely related to real and legitimate intellectual issues. Inevitably, however, personal idiosyncrasies added pepper to the debate.

Frequently differences of opinion were translated into issues of academic organization. I myself encountered an example of this, in the decision taken at Ben Gurion University in the mid-1970s to unify the Departments of Jewish and General History. This decision was one of the reasons I left Ben Gurion University. As I discovered while I was in the United States, the same issue crops up there, too.

Questions relating to the intellectual boundaries of Jewish studies were likely to jump up suddenly at international conferences. In the mid-1980s I participated in an international symposium at Tegersee, in Bavaria, on German-Jewish historical writing. Everything was proceeding smoothly when, toward the end, a debate literally erupted about how Jewish, or how German,

German-Jewish history actually was. What was most remarkable about the discussion was that it was generated by Israelis. The German scholars looked courteously astonished, while Jewish colleagues from Europe and America listened with almost sardonic expressions on their faces, as if to say: "Here are the Israelis again at their perennial quarrels!" I thought the discussion was very legitimate. After all, the continuing effort to define the equilibrium between Jewish and general components in Jewish life is a central problem in the search for a modern Jewish identity.

I was sometimes bemused by the way many of our Jewish colleagues from other institutions reacted to our disputations— and to our work in general. In my view, the debate just mentioned, or similar ones, signified the intellectual vitality that existed in our faculty, even if the discussions did sometimes become rather acerbic. However, we seemed to rub a raw nerve among many of our Jewish colleagues. I often heard Jewish friends who taught at other institutions relating salty descriptions of the quarrels, real and imaginary, as well as the intellectual and moral deficiencies, to be found at the Hebrew University. Obviously, if they did this in front of me, in my absence it could only be worse. But I soon found a way to stop it: "Indulging again in some Jerusalem-baiting?" I would ask, with the friendliest nastiness I could manage.

In truth, we sometimes added fuel to the fire. For instance, we frequently referred to the "Jerusalem school" of research in Jewish history. I did not then and I do not now know what exactly that phrase means. The term, apparently, has a chiefly symbolic meaning. It refers to some main trend of work on Jewish history (and probably also other fields of Jewish studies) which was and is shared by a large number of scholars—many in Jerusalem, many in other Israeli universities or throughout the Jewish world. But the very mention of the concept—Jerusalem school—caused such indignation, such flaring of tempers among my non-Jerusalemite interlocutors, that I kept repeating it, fascinated by the animus it provoked.

The effort to reach what was thought to be the right intellectual balance between the Jewish and non-Jewish cultural influences that had shaped the work of our predecessors at the Hebrew University did not lose any of its force in my own generation. In addition to the factors mentioned above, the changes going on in Israeli society created new questions and gave the issue a new pungency. When I began my studies, socialist Zionism, with its emphasis on secular culture and social achievement, was still one of the leading ideological values in Israeli society. During the late 1960s and into the 1970s, however, the Socialist-Zionist ethos lost much of its ideological weight. New influences, especially those which were more traditionally Jewish and/or more nationalistic, began to assert themselves. The question of religion emerged in Israeli life with a new and, for me, surprising vitality. These social and intellectual currents were felt in all walks of Israeli life, and they created their own new background of dilemmas and pressures for those of us in academia.

However, I think we have dealt with the challenge successfully. More than once I have heard sarcastic observations from colleagues, even those teaching at the Hebrew University, about the high proportion of teachers in the Department of Jewish History who were religious Jews, i.e., orthodox religious. Though the fact is correct, the implication that an orthodox point of view was now prevalent is totally unfounded. In spite of the growing influence of orthodox people and issues in the city of Jerusalem, the Hebrew University continues to be an island of intellectual openness and tolerance. On Mount Scopus, at least, synagogue and state remain well separated.

ᆼᆼ

In such an intellectual and human environment, the people I appreciated most were those who combined a high level of academic excellence with an equally high degree of personal stability. I shall mention only a few, whom I came to know well.

Corpulent and totally bald, Menahem Stern looked like a benevolent Buddha. He was the sanest person I have ever known. Indeed, he generated around him a mood of spiritual equilibrium that influenced everybody who came in contact with him. Stern was a superb scholar—his academic field was Jewish history in the Second Temple period—with an unrivalled knowledge of classical sources. None of the many human foibles of the Hebrew University in general, and of the Institute of Jewish Studies in particular, seemed to touch Menahem. He also had an unsurpassed sense of the practical, and was the last man to be obfuscated by the numerous superficial commotions of academic life. I remember a heated debate in the Department of Jewish History about a new bibliography to be prepared for the students. Menahem sat aside, silent, obviously bored. When somebody remembered to ask for his opinion, his reaction was typical: "But what about the old book-list? Have the students already finished reading it?" Another time, when we both were discussing some intricate matter of academic policy, he suddenly stopped and said: "Now, let us talk about something of real importance. What is happening with your academic promotion?"

Stern's end is one of the most terrible of my Jerusalem recollections. He, the most peaceful of men, was assassinated in the early 1990s by two Arab terrorists. It happened in the middle of the morning, while he was walking from his home to the university library. He took the same route every day, and perhaps they had been stalking him. His tragic death haunts my imagination. He was probably deeply engrossed in some historical issue of centuries ago and never grasped exactly what those two knive-wielding men wanted from him.

Thin and withered, Jacob Katz looks like a sparrow. Indeed, he has been looking the same, with approximately the same ninety pounds of flesh and bones since I first met him, some thirty-five or forty years ago. Nevertheless, it would not surprise me to hear that he still enjoys excellent health. Katz is an international authority on Modern Jewish history, and he was one of the first to introduce sociological categories into this field of research, although basically he remained a historian. While I was a student, I participated in one of his courses. Unfortunately, because of some silly incident related to an in-class lecture that I should have delivered differently, we remained mutually cool for the next two decades—very typical of human relations in the Hebrew University. In later years, Joseph Salmon, a close friend and colleague from my Beer Sheva days who had been a former student of Katz, brought us together again. We met, and I left with a bittersweet aftertaste: sweet, because the conversation was so congenial; bitter, because it had taken so long to realize the wealth of professional good sense and historical wisdom I could have taken advantage of, but did not.

Katz's career at the Hebrew University was far from easy. It started late, and his position was split between two faculties and three departments, or something like that—he used to laugh about it in later years, but it cannot have been a laughing matter at all. Katz's first important work, *Tradition and Crisis*, published in Hebrew in the late 1950s, was severely criticized by Ettinger and by his close colleague and friend, Haim Hillel Ben-Sasson, which had not made Katz's life any easier.

114

What impresses me most about Katz is his intellectual vitality. In his late eighties, Katz remained original and academically productive. Despite his age, he was able to listen to and consider some new and outrageous historical idea with the open-mindedness of a teenager. However, there was in Katz a dimension I never understood entirely: although he was an extremely Orthodox Hungarian Jew (and Orthodox Hungarian Jews are the most extreme of all), he was endowed with an absolute independence of mind and judgment. Among the teachers I have known at the Hebrew University there were few like Katz, or Stern, in whose proximity (others would say, under whose protection) one could work with total intellectual liberty. Although they might not offer the fierce, sometimes overwhelming, intellectual stimulation one experienced in Ettinger's environment, they fostered a more detached, calmer atmosphere of intellectual freedom.

Sergio DellaPergola belongs to a younger generation of Hebrew University faculty. His field is statistics and demography, especially Jewish demography. Sergio looks the Italian he is: a Mediterranean type, well-dressed (a rarity at the Hebrew University), courteous, with a well-modulated voice. The impact of his powerful intellect is carefully low-keyed, but how powerful it is! I first came in close contact with him while working on my *Atlas of Modern Jewish History;* initially he did not make much of an impression on me. DellaPergola played around with the complexities of demographic knowledge with such ease that for a moment I, the clumsy historian, had the illusion that I really understood what it was all about. Behind his prowess with statistical categories lurks a fine humanistic sensibility. Sergio was unfailingly helpful to me, and generous with his ideas. Under his ever discreet guidance I underwent a crash-course in the essentials of demographic work and logic that went on for weeks and months. Looking back, it is obvious to me that without DellaPergola's assistance I would have committed countless mistakes in the compilation of that *Atlas*. Obvious to *me*—Sergio never even hinted at the importance of his help.

One relationship I hesitate to summarize is with Elieser Schweid—not because it is so difficult, but because it is so close. As I have mentioned already, Sabina and Eli Schweid were my first acquaintances in Jerusalem: when I settled in Jerusalem, in 1955, I rented a room in the house where they were (and still are) living, on that hill in Abu Tur, overlooking the Old City. Since then we have remained very good friends. I consider Eli the most important intellectual active today in Israeli life. Eli's academic and intellectual-public interests frequently overlapped, unlike those of the other people I have mentioned: Menahem Stern, because he was too skeptical regarding public matters; Jacob Katz, probably because his position was too complex. (However, it was Katz who said, during one of David Ben Gurion's controversial periods in the late 1950s, that Ben Gurion, like the weather, should be regarded as an unavoidable affliction of nature.)

Eli Schweid is attracted and fascinated by the greatest of all themes: the unending complexities of the evolving spiritual foundations of the new Israeli society, the difficult evolution of a Jewish identity which combines age-old Jewish elements with the new experiences of Israeli life. He has observed and commented on that process through the sophisticated lens of his academic calling, modern Jewish thought. Schweid's work on the role of religion in a Jewish state, on the relationship between Israel and the Jewish Diaspora, on the future of the Diaspora itself, on the spiritual characteristics of the developing Israeli society, is of seminal importance. Here, however, I have had a problem. On the one hand, I respect Eli's academic work very much—with a touch of envy, because he has that rare gift of being able, while working on a theme, to produce a first written draft that is practically definite. On the other hand, I cannot remember a single case where I have not had some reservation regarding his ideas about present-day intellectual issues, and sometimes I have disagreed with him completely. That in spite of this we have remained such good friends only shows what a generous man Eli Schweid is.

All the men I have mentioned here could not have been more dissimilar. In their origins and their personal makeup, they collectively represent the completely disparate human composition of Israeli society. Nevertheless, they have much in common, besides their intellectual brilliance. These are all men of strong character and personal integrity, steeled by the not-always-easy and frequently frustrating conditions of academic life at the Hebrew University. All have been generous and human, *mentshlekh*. All share a quality that is uncommon in Israeli (and other) life: the capacity to criticize somebody's ideas, even reject them entirely, without personally offending the man or woman involved. Curiously, there is another thing, a small but in my opinion highly indicative one, which they have in common: they always make time for others. Although they have all been very productive intellectually—which means, hard-working—if I asked to talk with them, they would generally see me the same day, or the day after. It has become my belief that professors or intellectuals who make "appointments" for two weeks later are either lazy, or poorly organized, or snobs.

⬥

I have been asked if I am "happy" at the Hebrew University. I frown: first, because I do not care for that kind of question; second, because I am not. I would not even mention it, but for the fact that I share the feeling with quite a number of colleagues—some of them very successful scholars, men and women who have no patience for self-pity, and who have been associated with the Hebrew University since the beginning of their academic careers. Some attribute their mood to a decline in the quality of the students. I smile: it reminds me of the story I read once about a professor at the Sorbonne who thundered against his students, a bunch of radicals and drunkards, interested only in wine and women—not at all like the students of his own generation, who had been sober and serious. The complaint was, I think, made in 1461—or was it 1561? I do not dare to say it loudly, but my impression is that students today are better than in my time. They surely have a harder life: to begin an academic career in the 1990s seems much more difficult than it was thirty years ago.

Although the Hebrew University has certainly been a very adequate place to work, congenial it is not. I was much more "at home" at Ben Gurion University, in spite of my disappointing end there. However, my ambivalent feelings may reflect the benefits of being associated with the Hebrew University: one should not expect comfort on a hill where so many winds blow. The same is true for political parties or large corporations. The Hebrew University is not a place to relax, but to work—even to struggle. Beneath the veneer of genteel academic activity loom the uneasiness, the questions, the challenges of a vigorous culture.

16

The Simplicities and Complexities of Historical Work

As mentioned before, there had been a moment, in the earlier stages of my academic career, when I pondered whether to specialize in Jewish or European history. In terms of my personal development, I was better prepared for the latter direction. I made my choice while participating in a course given by Joshua Prawer on medieval European history. His theme was the life and customs of medieval knights, and Prawer's description and analysis were systematic and interesting. However, they did not interest me enough, those knights and their mores.

I opted for Jewish history, for the modern period. Although I have enjoyed my work very much, I cannot imagine another theme in modern humanistic sciences so permeated with tension, so permanently demanding of one's spiritual resources. Actually, it was that inner tension that attracted me, but some time passed before I understood its diverse components. Mainly, they are three: the first, which I mentioned in the preceding chapter, is the ambiguity of the modern Jewish condition, searching for a balance between Jewishness and cultural attachment to the Gentile world. The second component has to do with the after-effects of the Holocaust, a theme I shall return to. The third component is the deeply ingrained ideological character of Israeli society.

In one sense, Israeli society is extremely open with regard to the exchange of ideas. Not because it is very tolerant (which it is not), but because its bewildering Jewish ethnic and religious variety creates a situation where everybody may say or write anything. This openness, however, functions principally on the broad level of Israeli society as a whole. On the next, lower level, where each Israeli lives and works in his or her own social and cultural sphere, the rules are subtly different. Ideas are not formally imposed on the individual, but there are generally accepted concepts of enormous impact, which I have termed "the sacred cows of the Israeli national ideology."

There are quite a few of these "sacred cows." I mentioned earlier how Me'ir Vereté finished off one of them, the myth of the Balfour Declaration. There are many others. One time I ran into complications at quite an early stage of my work with the concept of the "Zionist revolution." Who dared to doubt that Zionism was a revolutionary development in modern Jewish life?

It gradually became clear to me that Zionism is an amalgam of several ideological concepts, one of which is not revolutionary at all, but deeply traditional and rooted in centuries of Jewish history and consciousness: the idea of *hibbat-tzion*, meaning the love-for-Zion, or the yearning-for-Zion. I became convinced that the yearning-for-Zion component is more important than the other ideological elements that are part of modern Zionism, such as antisemitism and nationalism. Incidentally, I became more and more doubtful about the significance of antisemitism. It seemed to me that modern antisemitism drove Jews to America, not to Palestine. However, I felt more comfortable explaining my point of view in English: in Hebrew, the ideological conditioning of the language (*mahapeha tzionit*, "Zionist revolution") is so strong that one is carried along by it. It is as if the language itself thinks for one, and acts as an ideological buffer against any heterodox view.

A similar situation exists with regard to another theme, the relationship between the Holocaust and the creation of the Jewish state in 1948. *Hurban Utekuma* (destruction and rebirth, in English) are concepts that in Hebrew are interlocked and self-evident. But what occurs if one comes to believe that there is *no* direct relationship between *Hurban* and *Tekuma*, between the Holocaust of European Jewry and the establishment of Israel?

This is an opinion I arrived at in the late 1970s. My argument followed two lines of thought. First, the United Nations decision in November 1947 to partition Palestine was the result of international political interests that were essentially unrelated to the destruction of European Jewry. Second, from a Zionist point of view the creation of Israel resulted from the long-range positions of Zionist ideology and the short-term reaction to the 1939 White Paper. That last document effectively put an end to the Zionist-British relationship founded on the Balfour Declaration of 1917. To accept the 1939 White Paper would have meant agreeing to a Palestinian state dominated by a two-thirds Arab majority that was violently anti-Zionist. Since a national movement does not commit suicide, the Zionists had turned to the only alternative: Jewish political independence in Palestine—before the facts about Hitler's systematic destruction of European Jewry became known.

This was a provocative thesis, counter to prevailing opinion. However, there was little reaction to the article when I managed to have it published, with much difficulty, first in English (1979), later in Hebrew (1980). Then in the early 1980s I was invited to participate in a televised discussion of the relation between the Holocaust and the establishment of Israel. "Professor, with all due respect, this is not your classroom, this is TV. You've got exactly four minutes to state your case!" In those few minutes I tried to explain the main lines of the concept. When the program was aired two weeks later, I was able to watch my own performance: unfamiliar with the medium, I looked unsure and sounded unconvincing. However, the moment the program ended, the telephone started to ring and did not stop for an entire week. People came up to me on the street, to agree, to disagree. It was a powerful and a worrisome demonstration of the influence of television.

Had I really managed, on that issue, to open a hole in the wall of received wisdom regarding that issue? I wonder. A new idea is like a tender sapling; in most cases it does not survive the rough weather of established opinion. If it does, if a new view succeeds in putting out roots, growing, extending branches, becoming accepted by public or academic opinion, it is very difficult to understand how the process actually happens. People are basically conservative in their thought, even those whose profession it is to devise and evaluate new ideas. I always found it very difficult to publish an article whose leading idea did not conform to established norms. Each essay I wrote on the themes mentioned above was rejected several times, both in English and in Hebrew, before I found someone (and sometimes literally tricked someone) who would publish it. Eventually I developed a rule of thumb: if an article of mine was accepted without discussion, it might be because it was based on solid research or illuminated a new historical point. Highly original it was not.

There were deeper lessons to be drawn from those episodes as well. On the surface, the professional tools of the historian appear to be simple ones: what is the focus of the discipline, beyond careful use of documents from the past? Indeed, in an era of scientific specialization, many of my colleagues have become uneasy with the supposed simplicity of the historical method compared to other professions; they literally try to complicate our work. They have introduced complex computer programs and employed sophisticated methods of statistical analysis. During discussions about certain historical research projects, one may hear the comment: "Oh, this is something we do not have enough scientific knowledge about. We should call a sociologist." Or perhaps a political scientist, a psychologist, an anthropologist.

Although my instinct tells me that little is to be gained from such worthies, I usually give way, mainly to avoid appearing narrow-minded. However, I do not remember a single case where the sociologist or the psychologist in question helped me to crack a major historical conundrum. They were able to clarify subsidiary matters, but they usually brought confusion to central ones, and altogether much time was lost on both sides. I do not mean that the tools of other scientific fields are of no use for historical work: on the contrary. But the historian must learn to use these tools and adapt them to the discipline. It is a difficult challenge, and few people have managed to do it well.

Why is that so? Because, I came to understand, the alleged simplicity of the historical method is an illusion. Two factors make historical work extremely complex: one is methodological, the other intellectual. Shmuel Ettinger taught me that the apparent simplicity of the historical method is deceptive. Beyond pains taking evaluation of documents, he stressed, one must learn that "good" history is a delicate equilibrium between knowledge acquired through objective research of historical material and subjective value judgments regarding the historical issue being examined. All the professional railings against subjectivity in historical work only show limited understanding of the discipline, insisted Ettinger, and I listened with astonishment. Was this not the opposite of what my other mentor, Israel Halperin, had insisted upon? But Ettinger certainly had a point: historical writing inevitably focuses on a handful of facts—a few out of millions. Historians must recognize the particularities of the facts they have chosen to concentrate on. I came to realize that true historical work reflects a right balance between objective craftsmanship and subjective perceptiveness. Good history means maintaining a good balance between both.

But what exactly does "subjective perceptiveness" mean? Here is another reason, an intellectual one, for the intricacy of work in history. Sooner or later a developing historian must adopt an intellectual viewpoint regarding his themes. Beyond choosing a certain field in historical work—cultural, social, economic or whatever—he must find an approach that will enable him consistently to identify and assemble those single-facts-among-millions on which he will construct his historical picture. In a narrow ideological or spiritual environment, a disciplinary viewpoint may be imposed on the young researcher from above, by his academic establishment or by an autocratic mentor. Ideally, one reaches it on one's own, through trial and error. Ideally, that search will involve a great deal of effort toward spiritual self-knowledge. It took me some time to reach and recognize my own approach, although this viewpoint had quite consistently directed my work almost from the beginning. In the 1980s, in the memoirs of American journalist and writer Theodore H. White, *In Search of History,* I found what I consider my own position expressed more clearly than I could ever do:

He had been a mild Marxist at one time in his youth because that was the fashion of his generation. . . . And then had come home to American politics and begun to see it as an adventure in which men sought their identity. . . ."
Though he could not give up that old thought entirely, he knew it was insufficient to explain politics. Identities in politics, he now realized, were connected far more to ideas than to ego,

123

to id, or to glands. At the core of every great political identity lay an idea—an idea imposed on the leader from his past, which the leader absorbed, changed and then imposed on the others outside. . . . The men he had since reported in politics were all the vessels of ideas. The armies, the navies, the budgets, the campaign organizations they commanded flowed from the ideas that shaped them, or the ideas they could transmit and enforce.

I, too, had come to recognize that at the root of any and every historical development lay an idea. Not an idea in the sense of a thought that had occurred to someone, but as a concept distilled through the accumulation of history. As much as human behavior (of individuals, of groups) is influenced by interests, those interests always move in some ideological frame. Historical figures or movements usually have no clear perception about the ideas that give meaning to and stimulate their activities. It is the historian's task to discover and analyze them, to explain the fascinating interplay of idea and interest that make sense of personal or collective behavior. It does not matter whether the contingencies of a given theme are examined in terms of cultural, political or demographic history.

ॐ

So far in this chapter I have focused on the study of history. Yet, it is obvious that historical work shares intellectual characteristics with scientific inquiry in general. I want to emphasize two of them: first, what I would call "creative innocence"; second, plain common sense.

Creative innocence means the capacity to look at a historical issue with the eyes of a child, unencumbered by prejudice and a priori knowledge. One should face each new historical question (or for that matter, any scientific issue) with wonder: "Now, isn't that incredible? How could that have happened?" Besides being vital for any learned inquiry, creative innocence may also neutralize one harmful limitation of the historical calling, conservativism. Historians tend to be conservative; it is almost an occupational disease. We have learned that most revolutions are shallow. We have too often seen that good ideas become corrupted. We have realized that men are willing to oppress in the name of freedom and to kill for the sake of life. Historians learn to revere tradition, those values that hold a society together and give it its identifiable character. However, this tendency must be kept under a tight rein. One should never forget that tradition blooms only when challenged. Left to itself, tradition may all too quickly degenerate into the Inquisition.

True, when analyzing history one cannot ignore those more "settled" aspects of human behavior, such as tradition, experience, historical knowledge. Yet in fact, they stand in the way of "innocent" questioning. After all, has not everything already happened before? Personally, I have always been wary of experience. I have never met a man or a woman whom experience has made any better, or wiser, or more lovable. On the contrary, it is exactly the people who have not let themselves be bent by their life experiences who are the most admirable. Men or women with that peculiar "experienced" look in their eyes have usually been smart from birth.

If, however, I query experience, does this mean that I draw no lessons from our historical studies, none that can make our future behavior more rational? Are we condemned to repeat the mistakes of the past, plus some new ones, until the end of time? There is, undoubtedly, something like collective experience—we may call it historical experience—but its characteristics are nebulous, and the ways in which it accumulates, even more so. How to benefit from it, how to draw "lessons" from it, seems to be beyond our human capabilities.

There is no place like Israel to learn some sobering realities about the limitations of so-called historical experience. Israeli public opinion, about the freest and most vigorous I have met anywhere, is split right down the middle regarding that most basic of our political problems: how to deal with the Palestinians and the Arabs. The survival of Israel—nothing less—is the ultimate issue at stake. Would it most surely be guaranteed by filling the West Bank with Jewish settlements as quickly as possible—even if that means endless confrontations and exhausting Israel's limited resources? Or would the ultimate goal be better served by the opposite policy, letting the Palestinians go their way and develop whatever institutions they want, and by paying the price some Arab states are demanding in return for accepting a Jewish state in the Middle East? Even when it is clear that some of the Arab states are opposed to any dialogue whatsoever with the "Zionist entity" (Arabese for Israel)? Historical knowledge and experience add only a small measure to the dimensions of these questions. One could know all of history, past and present, and still be unable to resolve these issues.

Since there are so many intrinsic complexities in the study of history, one cannot proceed without common sense. Any given historical event might have occurred for a myriad possible reasons and causes, and one can always find documents supporting the most outlandish possibilities. Historical work may be done from diverse points of view and angles. They are all legitimate, as long as one remains attuned to what the Germans call *Sitz im Leben,* the life setting. This does not always happen, as I came to think from the example of psycho-history.

In the 1970s, I was invited to a friend's home for a meeting with a scholar who combined psychoanalytical training with historical research, and who told us about his work. His theme was the political conduct of Otto Bauer, one of the leaders of the Austrian Social-Democratic movement in the interwar period. Bauer had played a tragic role in the events of the late 1920s and 1930s, failing to stand up against the right-wing political coalitions that eventually overturned the Austrian democracy.

Regarding sources for a psycho-historical study of Bauer, there had been a windfall. Freud's famous patient "Dora," whose treatment was of great importance in the development of Freud's ideas, was none other than Ida Bauer, Otto's sister. From what was known about the circumstances of Dora's case, and from additional personal material, it was possible to build a psychoanalytical model of the relationship between Otto Bauer and his parents. It turned out that between an obsessional mother and a deficient father figure, Bauer had developed a neurotic personality. He was torn by feelings of guilt, and he lacked initiative in situations of political crisis. Our specialist argued that Bauer's psychological background explained his much too prudent political approach to events in 1927 and 1933, when the confrontation between the Austrian socialists, on the one hand, and political-clerical and right-wing groups, on the other, resulted in the defeat of the Social Democrats.

Was Otto Bauer an isolated phenomenon? Our lecturer believed that there were strong similarities between Bauer and several other leaders of European Social-Democratic parties in the interwar years: middle-class Jewish intellectuals, brilliant theoreticians who had behaved poorly in situations of political upheaval. Our psycho-historian wrapped himself in his professional trappings like a medieval monk in his habit. His thesis, he declared, was only speculative, no more than "exploratory." He solicited

our reactions to further work. The terms "perhaps," "it is possible," "one of the factors," "certainly not the only reason," were
repeated with the precision of a Japanese tea ceremony. But at the
end, a question remained floating in the air: could it be that the
psychological diversions (or perversions) of those middle-class,
Jewish, socialist leaders explained—perhaps, possibly, was only
one factor among many, etc., etc.—the failure of European Social
Democracy between the world wars?

I was appalled by the lack of common sense in the thesis:
should one not suppose, I asked, that among the opponents of
Austrian Social Democracy—or, for that matter, among all the
fascists, clericals, communists and whatever else in Europe—
there were thousands, even millions, with a psychoanalytical
makeup similar to Otto Bauer's? Later on I spoke about this with
a close friend, Joseph Sandler, an outstanding authority in psychoanalytical theory. It is difficult to imagine a more appropriate
person to listen to my doubts. Sandler had helped me in a tough
personal situation; I knew that besides his high level of theoretical insight he was blessed with a very practical turn of mind. He
shrugged his shoulders: "Common sense is something one is
born with. No university has yet developed a 'common sense
course,' " was his comment.

Over the years I have heard or read psycho-historical studies
of Napoleon, Hitler (his mother's sufferings at the hands of a
Jewish doctor, who became a substitute figure for his hated father, had stimulated Hitler's antisemitism), several biblical figures, and so on. From any viewpoint of historical judgment, it
was all irrelevant. There is an abyss between personal behavior
and social, historical events which psycho-history cannot bridge.
Worse, many psycho-historians seem unaware and unwilling to
see that their ideas are simply senseless. Psychoanalysis is a serious calling, and so is history. Put them together as has been done
so far, and the result seems to me a sophisticated edition of "Trivial Pursuit."

∾

In the end, what may be gained from the study of history?
Quite a number of things, some more significant, some less. One
is that human beings were not more stupid in the past than they
are today. Their actions, right or wrong, have not always
stemmed from their lack of wisdom, but rather from the character

of their social institutions and spiritual environments, and the circumstances of their particular human condition. We are not smarter, or better, than our ancestors.

History can also teach us that life is neither tidy nor logical, and that we should accept this state of affairs. Indeed, I have learned to be suspicious of people, historians or otherwise, who try to sell me a precisely ordered or neatly packaged view of some event. I have never been disconcerted when someone jumps up and asserts:

"But sir, there is a contradiction in your explanation!" My standard response is:

"Life is a contradiction. Man is born to die: can there be a greater contradiction?"

Furthermore, one should learn from history to be careful about the lure of extremes. Far from what the Romantics believed, life and truth (another "sacred cow") are not identical or even harmonious; it frequently happens that they are in conflict. Therefore one should be suspicious about bearers of "The Truth," about fanatics with gleaming eyes and glittering messages. Too often they have been all too ready to kill for what they considered right. It is always so easy, so intoxicating to let oneself be drawn to extreme positions—of the left or the right, of this religious persuasion or that national principle—and so deadly. It is much more difficult, unrewarding, and seemingly boring to reach a middle-ground—a position that is not the result of passivity, but of level-headed consideration of diverse options.

And yet this kind of sober discernment must be balanced by a contradictory awareness: if humanity ever outgrew primitivism it happened because of extreme ideas, promulgated by wild-eyed thinkers, discoverers and preachers of truths who may have sounded preposterous, outrageous or even dangerous. The significance of human life, human achievement, human hope depends on the ideas underlying human endeavors. Those ideas have contributed to the slow distillation of historical experience which, for better or worse, has put mankind on its feet. Real, saving collective wisdom, in whose formation historical experience has certainly played a part, established a pattern of behavior that combined some measure of spiritual freedom with some measure of social balance.

Last but not least, history teaches us that this kind of wisdom is not a single peak to be conquered once. It is a quality that

is forever being attained and then lost, generation after generation, in an effort that should, and will, go on to the end of time.

∾

History is an important instrument for intellectual libera-
tion. We tend to believe that the values and institutions govern-
ing our lives and conditioning our thinking are permanent and
inviolable. History helps us to understand the relativity of it all,
and justifies the continuing search for something better. For
instance, it has been an ever-recurring pleasure for me to see the
light in the eyes of my better students when I explain that there
is nothing permanent or sacrosanct about the "state." When
they grasp that in its modern form the state is a relatively new
concoction—and one of the cruelest inventions with which man
has plagued himself. When they consider the possibility that the
sooner we manage to neutralize the all too powerful idea of the
modern state and establish efficient controls and boundaries
against its encroachments in our lives, the better off we will be.

Historical knowledge is a powerful instrument for our present self-understanding: our behavior, our values, our institutions, our problems. It aims to establish a measure of order in
the chaos of our existence and to create the sense of meaningful
continuity that is so essential to each reflective human being.
Indeed, as Rudyard Kipling put it, "The hours, the days and the
seasons, order their souls aright."

But these are also the limits of historical knowledge. With
each day, life dawns anew.

17

Oxford, 1985

Many of my ideas about history and historical work are the result of a very reflective period, the time I spent in Oxford, in 1984–85.

It was a difficult year. I had come to Oxford as a fellow of the Centre for Postgraduate Hebrew Studies. I lived in Yarnton—a village six miles outside the city, in the direction of Woodstock—in a well-preserved, sixteenth-century manor house owned by the Centre. The adjacent houses had also been modernized and converted into living quarters for visiting scholars. I was given large and comfortable lodgings, quite beyond my needs, since most of the time my family was not with me. I should have lived in town and not isolated myself in what was almost the country-side. In addition, personal circumstances weighed heavily. Almost without my being aware of it, my marriage was gradually dissolving. My wife and children came over for visits, but the cloud over our family life grew increasingly darker. Everyone in my family was suffering in his or her own way under the strain of the situation.

I had come to Oxford with a precise academic aim: to reach a better understanding of British motivations during their domination of Palestine, from 1917 to 1948. While preparing a book on Zionist policy (published in 1977), I was struck by the odd relationship between the British and the Zionists. They had some common goals in Palestine—or did they? They had acted together—or was it only side by side? Their interests in the country had slowly diverged over the years—but why was it such a protracted process? The British never had any trouble sloughing off a political pledge that no longer squared with their interests—witness the Sykes-Picot Agreement of 1916: signed one year, already eroding the next. Something had kept the British bound, or half-bound, to their commitment to the Zionists long after it became evident that the "real-political" usefulness of the Zionists was over. The causes of British indecisiveness deserved to be understood better. They certainly were an important ingredient of what came to be known as "the Palestine problem." And they were one of the important reasons behind the British debacle in Palestine in 1947–48.

I sensed a significant historical theme. If the British Empire had been created in a bout of absentmindedness, as the dictum popular among English historians went, the dictum hardly applied to Palestine. British policy there had been inspired—and later constrained—by deep-rooted motivations. There was a long history of interest in the Holy Land. At some point, as diverse scholars had already observed, the connection between the Jews and Palestine dawned on the consciousness of certain British groups. It was all rather obscure, but these ideas, seeping through the British social and religious establishment, had apparently played a part, perhaps a consequential one, in the maturation of the Balfour Declaration. The situation was strange, and its implications had been understood well—although in a negative way—by Elizabeth Monroe, the doyenne of post-war British historians of the Middle East: "Measured by British interests alone, it [the Balfour Declaration] was one of the greatest mistakes in our imperial history," she wrote in the early 1960s. If her judgment was devastating, it was not unperceptive: great historical mistakes are frequently driven by sound historical motivations.

My hope was to learn more about the inner workings of the British imperial mind. If British policy in Palestine had been related to some idea, Oxford was probably one of the breeding grounds where the seed of this idea had germinated. My intention was to work in British archives, especially in the Middle

East Centre of St. Antony's College, in the collections of the library of Rhodes House, and in London, in the Public Record Office. But first and foremost, I was looking for contact with British scholars pondering the same or similar issues. This, I was warned in advance, would not be easy. British reticence, or superciliousness, or snobbishness—the characterization depended on who offered the opinion—might make such contact difficult. To me it appeared an interesting, rather than a worrisome situation. Peculiar patterns of national behavior are always fascinating, and because of my personal background I adapt easily to them. I have also come to believe that behind the framework of collective manners and idiosyncrasies, people are basically quite similar. Individual men and women everywhere are driven by kindred impulses and interests; they are honest or dishonest, strong or weak, clever or foolish, in ways that are alike. Groups may behave and react according to their peculiar patterns—but the situation is different for individuals.

However, I was in for a rude surprise. My first contact with Oxford was like hitting a brick wall. It seemed as if I met no one. It was intriguing: while strolling through the well-tended quadrangles of the colleges, or reflecting in their exquisite chapels, my first impression was that something very important had happened in the place, but that the persons responsible were long gone. Later, when I became acquainted with some of my colleagues, Oxford acquired in my eyes a certain Jerusalem-like quality: there was a similar incongruity between the city and many of its present inhabitants. But if in Jerusalem, with time and patience, one could find one's place and make a connection with the environment, in Oxford this seemed not to work. Because I am a foreigner, I thought. But no, it appeared not to work with the English either. In fact, some English people appeared to have the most trouble of all with Oxford. Oxonian manners struck me as strained, their behavior affected. Their famed self-assurance impressed me as assumed rather than real. They behaved, I felt, as if they were acting in a theater play called Oxford.

I was also disappointed in my academic quest. British scholars were working on British policy in Africa, in Asia, even in the Middle East. But that peculiar chapter in British imperial history, the mandate period in Palestine, seemed to interest no one. Worse, I found a certain reluctance to deal with it, which was surprising, considering how apparently open-minded my

133

British colleagues were. There seemed to be a tacit understanding that everything on that theme had already been said—and what had not been was better left unmentioned, especially among gentlemen.

The search for a specific focus in historical quests is always uncertain. One may read heaps of documents and piles of books and articles, and never get anywhere. In the end, one will be led in a coherent direction less by the accumulation of all that wisdom than by an observation found in some document or the insight of a given scholar (not necessarily the most outstanding one). In my research work at Oxford, I found some guidance in the work of that strange person, James Morris. Morris was close to the British national tradition, but by virtue of being Welsh, he was also able to look at it from the outside. Morris's book on Oxford and his trilogy on the British Empire offered a wealth of insight into the British mentality and the ways it had shaped this city—and been shaped by it in turn. Morris's description of the formative importance of Oxford in Victorian times was convincing. Indeed, in the nineteenth century there was a close relationship between Oxford and the intellectual formation of the country's political elite and thus the imperial development of Great Britain. Oxford colleges were the source of many of the ideas that shaped the Empire and many of the men who ruled Great Britain's colonial possessions. The empire, explained Morris, set its imprint on Oxford, influenced its mentality, its behavior, its outlook on life and the world—and, in, turn, the university significantly shaped the empire.

The implicit conclusion was that the downfall of the British Empire had deeply affected Oxford. This point caused me some uneasiness. The common formulation, that "Great Britain had lost an empire but not yet found a new role," seemed to me shallow. It was reasonable to suppose that the empire was more a result than a cause of English history: cultural and economic factors had influenced the English national temper and social structure long before the imperial era. If there was an ethos in British public life in whose formation Oxford University had taken a leading part, its roots were probably laid down long ago. In the nineteenth century the British reaped the benefits of their past and recent history, among which was the thrust toward empire. Empire, then, was a harvest rather than a sowing. Furthermore, in spite of its breadth and power, the British Empire did not last long enough to be character-forming in the deeper national sense. It endured for barely a century. At its high point, the 1897 Jubilee, the economic basis that had made British expansion possible had already begun to erode.

Nevertheless, old habits die hard—historical habits even more so. The most resilient of all are imperial habits, it seems to me. Witness Spain, where imperial habits held on for ages, long after the great empire created in the sixteenth century had lost its meaning. To a lesser extent, something similar had apparently happened in England. The flowering of the imperial mentality and style had continued well into the twentieth century, when the foundations of the British Empire were dwindling away. The moment of truth arrived after World War II, and it was swift and devastating. In the space of twenty years the British lost most of their overseas possessions. Quite suddenly, Oxford's postures were out of tune with historical realities. The end of the empire caused an inner breakdown in the place that was so viscerally connected with its creation. Apparently I was witnessing something of the latter-day effects of that crisis.

But I was still not satisfied. What exactly did "Oxford" mean? My Jerusalem experience led me along a certain path of reflection. However differently people reacted to Jerusalem, everybody there seemed to share some common feeling in and about the city. Intellectuals were able to express, in their more sophisticated ways, perceptions that were sensed by people from all social groups, even those who were members of the various religious denominations and sub-denominations by which Jerusalem is blessed and cursed. In Oxford, diverse social classes reacted in completely unrelated ways. "Oxford blues," as I came to call them, referred to the melancholy of university scholars and those connected to them. The man in the grocery store, the woman in the post office, the automobile mechanic, the girl in the library—these people had no idea of and even less interest in the human and social phenomena I have been describing. In no place where I had so far lived had I sensed such a deeply ingrained class-separatedness as in Oxford—and mind, this was in the mid-1980s!

It appeared to me that the changed political circumstances of Great Britain had caused a greater crisis among the aristocracy and those sectors associated with it than among the broad masses of the British people. This did not make the post-empire period any less critical. Long ago I had come to recognize the importance of elite groups, social or intellectual, in shaping the larger human society. Examples abounded everywhere. In Israel, too, we had a telling case: the *kibbutz* movement. Although it represented only a tiny proportion of Israeli society, its members had been pivotal in the creation of the Jewish state. With regard to Great Britain, the empire had given the whole country a sense of collective pride. The source of the imperial impulse, however—its outlook on life and its patterns of behavior—was, in my view, the domain of a specific sector of British society. Oxford and Cambridge, together with the famous public schools that fed both with students, had been the intellectual and spiritual hothouses of that impulse. Thus the collapse of the empire drained much of Oxford's spiritual purpose. Great Britain, as the formulation went, may have lost an empire—but it was Oxford that had not yet found a new role.

How different the atmosphere in Oxford was from what I had experienced in the great American universities! The expansive intellectuals and political horizons of the American academic establishment were among my more powerful impressions of the United States. Even more than among American politicians or public officials, it was in the American academic establishment that one perceived an attitude almost imperial. There was an underlying sense that the world was their responsibility, the responsibility of America as seen by those professors. The world must be understood, helped, even manipulated—in short, be led. On a different level, while still a student I had noticed a corresponding phenomenon in the Hebrew University. Many of the older professors there, men of international standing and great dignity, had expressed a similar attitude of intellectual responsibility for the Jewish people.

Probably it had been that way in Oxford, too, a hundred or even fifty years ago. Now, however, the spirit was gone, and the place was but a shadow of former glories. Memories reverberated in chapels and quadrangles, but what remained was an empty shell, beautiful, keen on style, but powerless and rather sad. The reclusiveness of many English scholars, I came to understand, was due less to *hauteur* than to a sense of disorientation, even embarrassment. As intelligent men, they sensed their condition: they were no longer spokesmen for an outward-reaching ambition and ethos. They had become wardens of a museum.

Obviously, many of my impressions applied not only to Oxford but also to other English universities, and to the leading sector of English society. The difference was that in the hassle and hustle of London one paid scant attention to matters of national temper or the finer points of class mentality. Oxford, on the other hand, was an essentially reflective city. Like Jerusalem, it was a place that stimulated introspection.

My melancholic impressions were associated with situations that had a rather ludicrous side. The most typical Oxonian scholars I met were Sir Isaiah Berlin, the well-known philosopher and political scientist, and Peter Pulzer, Gladstone Professor of Government and Public Administration, both members of the very distinguished All Souls College. With their bony bodies, long faces, rich voices and impeccable accents, the two were embodiments of the stereotypical Oxford don. The catch was that the three of us might as well have spoken together in Yiddish: we were all Jews of Eastern European origin. Sir Isaiah even exercised on me the still quite passable Hebrew he had learned in his childhood! When I introduced myself (very formally) to Professor Pulzer, our conversation was so agreeable that I dared to ask him where he had been born.

"In Vienna," he answered.

Immediately my worst self took over, and I said in Yiddish: "Azoi, a Galitzianer!" (Many Viennese Jews had Galician roots, but preferred not to be reminded of it—though I am of Galician origin, and very proudly so).

"No, no" (hastily), "I am of Hungarian origin."

Well. . . .

ॐ

I gradually achieved some definition of the academic quest that had brought me to England: the trends underlying British policy in Palestine during the mandate. As mentioned above, several researchers had already drawn attention to the religious component in historic British attitudes regarding the Holy Land and the connection of the Jews with Palestine. The problem lay in explaining how such a nebulous spiritual interest had been transformed into a significant element of a political platform—as had happened with the Balfour Declaration. Furthermore, it was necessary to show how and in what ways that element had remained an active ingredient in British policy in Palestine from 1917 to 1948.

This was not a simple task: the British themselves had become quite confused about their presence and their motivations in Palestine. Their pragmatism made them less sensitive to obscure ties—perhaps religious, perhaps ideological—that bound their hands and directed their steps in Palestine onto paths they had trouble justifying. They found themselves enmeshed in a conflict between Jews and Arabs they had not anticipated. The history of the British in Palestine could be seen as a hesitant and unrewarding effort to find a middle ground between the clashing aspirations of Jews and Arabs. As one discerning British historian had noted, they found themselves sitting in the troublesome seat of Pontius Pilate. Gradually, however, the British had been drawn to the Arab side.

Yet I became convinced that throughout the mandate period the British had been influenced—or more precisely, had been constrained—by their original hard-to-define interest in the Jews and the Jews' connection to the Holy Land. Although it was only a vague idea, its roots went deep, and it proved quite resilient. Its substance had been grasped by such perceptive Zionists as Sokolow and, especially, Chaim Weizmann. They were talented enough to induce leading British public figures (who were half-convinced to start with) to associate the Zionists' hopes with their own political plans for Palestine. It took the British about thirty years to put aside that connection—enough time for the Zionists to lay the foundations of the Jewish state.

I tried to elaborate these ideas in a book (that was never finished) and in articles which appeared over the next few years. Here again I ran into difficulties. One of my main conclusions (received unenthusiastically by most of my Jewish colleagues) went against everything I had thought before on this theme. I was now convinced that in the political relationship which developed between the British and the Zionists, the British had been driven by an ideal, while the Zionists had been impelled by simple self-interest.

As I have tried to explain before, Zionism was a movement fed by powerful ideas. The internal history of modern Zionism—in the Diaspora, in Palestine and later in the State of Israel—constitutes one long, continuous struggle between ideological trends and sub-trends. In its political relationship with the British, however, there was almost no ideological dimension. To put it bluntly, the Zionists had used the British, rather than the British the Zionists.

That is, of course, an over-simplification, for the history of the British mandate in Palestine is filled with quirks and encumbered by contradictions. But it sums up the matter well. This thesis also offers an explanation for the subsequent disappointment of British historians and their severe condemnation of British policy in Palestine, culminating with Professor Monroe's judgment that the Balfour Declaration was "one of the greatest mistakes in [British] imperial history." The implicit question, for which present-day British historians offer no answer, was how such British statesmen as Balfour and Lloyd George, men admittedly clever and ruthless, could have committed such a tremendous error. The obvious answer is that it was not an error at all. Balfour and Lloyd George acted in their time according to one set of values, while latter-day historians (who, incidentally, should be familiar with the pitfalls of anachronism) base their evaluations on a completely different set of ideas. No one can say with confidence that Great Britain's situation in Palestine would not have been better, had the British held on to the original vision of Balfour and Lloyd George. The judgment of contemporary British historians dealing with mandatory Palestine is clouded by "Oxford blues," with a touch of (for the English) uncharacteristic national self-pity.

 basta

Altogether, my year in Oxford was a period of reasonable accomplishment, much thought, little joy, too much isolation. In the long English evenings I would go to nearby Woodstock and stroll through the gardens of Blenheim Palace, the ancestral abode of the dukes of Marlborough and Winston Churchill's birthplace. The color of the lake and hills changed through the evening, or became blurred by mist or light rain. I spent hours there trying to overcome my inner uneasiness, forcing myself to ponder my academic interest. The setting was certainly appropriate for such thoughts: redolent of past British imperialism and suggestive of the strange transformations in the British intellectual temper.

I left Oxford in September of 1985. It had rained almost the whole summer. The days were getting shorter, autumn and then winter would come soon—yet I had experienced practically no sunshine! I found this depressing, and I wondered how this climate influenced the English soul. Oxford is the only place where, after having spent a considerable time, I have little interest in going back. How did the Nazarene put it? "Let the dead bury their dead."

18

Israel as Experience

      Several years ago I had a student in one of my courses at the Hebrew University, Jean, a girl from England. Her behavior in class was frequently a problem: she was aggressive, bitingly ironic and with little patience (at times justifiably so) for the opinions of others. Her redeeming feature was her mind: a truly outstanding intelligence, burdening, rather than supporting, an unhappy personality. But it was a pleasure to talk to her; she had a sharp eye for the incongruities of Israeli reality which I found refreshing, although pitiless. I was not surprised when she decided to leave the country at the end of the semester, instead of remaining throughout the academic year.

      Three months later I was walking on Ben Yehuda street, in the center of Jerusalem, and whom should I meet? Jean!

      "Jean, what are *you* doing here? You were so glad to leave!"

      "Yes," she answered, "life is easier in England. But here it is more intense."

      But "intense" is not the right term. To live in Israel is like sitting on a volcano, an active one. There is almost no major plight of modern society that does not find here an inflated expression:

security problems with Arab states and Palestinian neighbors, the internal fissures of a population brought together—and still arriving—from all possible and impossible countries, tensions between secular and religious sectors, economic headaches, the cultural conundrum, the ecological mess. . . .

ᘎ

A useful rule in relation to public matters is to hold to the essentials and compromise about the rest. In Israel, however, that otherwise sensible principle has seemed to spark an astonishing amount of heat. Israelis argue forever about questions that hardly seem to deserve it. One might think that the debate is more important than the solution. For many it looks suspiciously like an exercise in Talmudic wit. But not to me. In a society of extremely varied composition, fairly democratic, where social and cultural patterns of behavior are still evolving; where no political position dominates a decisive part of the political spectrum; where the population functions on a relatively high intellectual and ideological level; and last but not least, where the problems are very real—public debate is unavoidably acerbic. Depending on the point at issue, opposing sectors of Israeli politicians may combine in bewildering alliances. Even if this phenomenon smacks of political opportunism, it also reflects an awareness about what is essential. The problem is that there are too many essentials in Israeli life, all different, most contradicting each other.

I tried once to order the problems of the Israeli reality not according to their importance (they all are), but by their urgency. At the bottom of my private list was the so-called "ethnic" issue, the adjustment of Jews from all the corners of the world to a common frame of life. A more or less integrated society *is* emerging in Israel. This is not happening because of the wisdom of some public masterplan. Quite the contrary. Deep-rooted historical tendencies in Jewish society (or societies), beyond the manipulating capabilities of our public sages, have produced these integrational patterns among Israelis. Never mind if the new Israeli society fell short of everyone's private expectations. The very fact that the process was happening is a miracle. The world is full of countries being torn apart because of ethnic tensions that stretch back to time immemorial. And here was Jewish society in Israel, coping quite successfully with the "ingathering of the exiles."

Quite successfully? There is a dimension in that "achieve-ment" that makes me shudder. Emigration to Israel brought an end to the cultural heritage of Jewries arriving from East and West. Some people have managed to convince themselves that the diverse Jewish cultures were being "amalgamated" into a new Israeli blend. But to me it appeared they were simply being crushed, that a whole treasure of old and proud Jewish creation—the result of generations of work, study and life—was being sucked into the whirlpool. There is an immanent cultural brutal-ity in that process, the emergence of the new Israeli society.

Although many of us are aware of this, full recognition of the process involves a wrenching effort. And what can be done, beyond pondering with a heavy heart? Besides, has something similar not happened in every society undergoing moderniza-tion? Was I not being deluded by romantic nostalgia for a past that probably was far from ideal, and which was inexorably due to change? Such change was unavoidable, it belonged to the nature of things. I remembered the words of the Jewish historian Simon Dubnow, written in 1911:

Every generation in Israel carries within itself the remnants of worlds created and destroyed during the course of the previous history of the Jewish people. The generation, in turn, builds and destroys worlds in its form and image, but in the long run contin-ues to weave the thread that binds all the links of the nation into the chain of the generations. . . . Thus each generation in Israel is more the product of history than it is its creator. Each individ-ual member of a generation, who is not like a dry branch or a leaf fallen from the tree, carries the "burden of the heritage" of the chain of generations; and he carries it willingly or unwillingly, knowingly or unknowingly. He is nursed and fed by the national forces accumulated in the past even when he rebels against the very means through which the forces were accumulated and even when he strives to destroy them, or to alter their form, or "reform" them.

Although Dubnow's view impressed me, it still seemed to me that what was happening in Israel was extremely rough. This was one reason why I always felt uncomfortable when asked to speak about Israeli culture. Objectively, I knew that compared to the modern level of cultural and scientific creation accomplished by Jews in all possible fields around the world, we in Israel were experiencing a phase of cultural disarray. Subjectively, I felt inhibited because I was asked to speak about cultural creation, yet I was more mindful of cultural collapse. True, as Dubnow had written, more than the creators of Jewish history, we were the product of it. But I wondered if we were continuing to weave that thread linking the generations, or if in our time it was being torn to shreds.

However, there certainly was a singular Israeli "experience," one of the most powerful and dramatic of our century. That experience, I hoped, would in the end yield a good harvest. It was a matter of time. Of time, work, patience. And continuing efforts toward honest self-appraisal.

There was another issue so far at the bottom of my list of Israeli problems that I became aware of it only when colleagues from abroad asked me about it: what my interlocutors called the "militarization" of Israel. It seems part of human nature to brush aside complications that could, that might develop, but do not. The situation of the military in Israel is an example of this. To the best of my knowledge, in no other country do defense and military matters occupy so large a part in the life of the state and its population. However, miracle of miracles, Israel has not become militarized. Foreign colleagues, especially those in the field of political science, found this hard to believe.

"If the United States kept an army of a size proportional to yours"—ran one argument—"we would have over thirty million citizens connected directly or indirectly to the armed forces. Would not the military then develop a significant measure of political power? And you want me to believe that in Israel, a less experienced democracy than ours, your army does not influence your political life?"

"Indeed, this is the situation in Israel. No influence."

"And what about all those generals occupying ministerial positions in the government? Members of your parliament? Those colonels in industry? In public administration? Even in the universities?"

"They are all retired. Ours is a young army. Most professional officers retire at forty and start a civil career. And in any case, the bulk of the army are the reservists. The Israeli army is truly an army of the people. It is impossible for an ambitious chief-of-staff to use the army to develop his personal political ambitions. He would find himself with very few followers and a huge camp of opponents."

My interlocutors seemed doubtful. I understood their disbelief: in this matter their usual intellectual guidelines were of little help. Past experience had taught them that when the military pushed its way into the political sector of a new country, one could reasonably expect dire consequences. So far, however, Israel is different.

Israeli military prowess is directly related to an issue that was high on my list of public worries, the Arab-Israeli conflict. As I saw it, there are two facets to the issue. One is the necessity of paying close, careful attention to the ongoing military confrontation with the Arab states—a matter about which Israelis are very conscious and fairly unified. The second facet is the need to break the dynamics of the confrontation, to alter the cycle of continuing escalation. This is the part of the world where we and the Arabs want to live, not to die. It is imperative to create some patterns of understanding, at least with those Arabs in contiguous areas, and especially with the Palestinians. A significant segment of Israeli society seemed to avoid looking at this side of the problem.

It would be correct to say that the two facets overlap: one can hardly talk about Arab or Palestinian rights without raising the issue of whether those rights contradict Israeli ones or impair our security. However, I frequently felt that I was being manipulated by some of my Israeli interlocutors: while they spoke with me about national security, among themselves the issue was how to guarantee more land in the occupied territories for Jewish settlement. In the ongoing debate among us Israelis, people like me who were truly looking for a compromise had weaknesses in our positions that our Jewish opponents were aware of. We knew (and they knew we knew) that no land in Palestine had ever been attained by the Jews without struggle. In addition, neither faction trusted the political Arab. If he was forthcoming, whom did he speak for? How could we be sure that what he agreed to would not be rejected by the next Arab? The problem can be represented by a closed circle, with no way out.

Because I am an academic, I was unavoidably drawn into the endless propaganda war between Israel and the Arabs. While I was abroad, I would frequently be asked to participate in some debate, colloquium, seminar or symposium about the "situation" in the Middle East, meaning the Israeli-Arab conflict. Usually the occasion involved a confrontation with some Arab representative. The debate itself went like a well-rehearsed play. We, the main actors, knew our own roles well, knew by heart also the lines of the other side. We had participated in that show many times (the play had already been around for more than forty years), and we behaved reasonably well. Most of the public had seen that presentation before, many more than once, and almost everybody held a definite opinion. After the debate my Arab opponent and I might have coffee together; on these occasions, surprisingly or not, the conversation usually loosened up. We managed to get beyond the clichés and bemoan together, quite sincerely, that no solution had been found to the Arab-Israeli conflict.

I was also amazed by how many of my Arab interlocutors claimed to be Jerusalemites. It seemed I met a whole Arab Diaspora from Jerusalem. Once, while teaching in the States, the dean of the faculty introduced me at a party to a Middle Eastern gentleman, the chairman of the Department of Arabic Language and Culture. Colleagues stood around, smiling tensely, hoping no unpleasantness would ensue. There seemed no danger. I was resolved to behave well, and the chairman had the perfect manners for which Arabs are well-known.

"What a pleasure, Professor Friesel! Welcome, welcome. . . . Where do you live in Israel?"

"In Jerusalem," I answered, rather baffled. I had been sure that he knew it.

"Oh, really. . . . How interesting! Actually, I am from Jerusalem, too!"

"How nice. . . . Do you know the city well?"

"Hmmm, yes; although, alas, many years have passed, many years. . . . Were you born in Jerusalem?"

"No, I came to Jerusalem when I was twenty-five years old."

"I was born in Jerusalem!"

"Hmmm. . . . I answered, noncommittally.

"Actually," continued the professor, "ours is a very old Jerusalemite family."

"Actually," I reacted at last, "ours is an ancient Jerusalemite family, too. It is only that we have just started that very old family."

Alas, that was the end of our conversation.

One of the outcomes of these recurring debates was that I become suspicious of Gentile sponsors or participants who claimed that theirs was an "objective" attitude toward the conflict and that they wanted to make a "fair" contribution to the debate. In too many cases they actually leaned to the Arab side and harbored obscure antisemitic feelings. Theoretically, both the Israeli and the Arab sides were right, and both were wrong. The only possible solution was the almost impossible one: Jews and Arabs must learn to live together, or side by side, while disagreeing. If a Gentile chose to put his head into such a dispute, he inevitably ended up identifying with one side or the other. And when this happened, he seldom recognized it honestly.

However, if both sides were at the same time right and wrong, were not many of the major arguments of both Arabs and Jews rather senseless? Actually, that was what I eventually came to recognize. One Zionist contention, frequently made since the beginnings of Jewish settlement in Palestine, was that the Jewish presence in Palestine would surely benefit the Arabs, since it would improve their social and economic condition. Considering how sophisticated Zionist ideology ordinarily was about its own aims, such reasoning sounded downright dumb. How would the Jews have reacted if they were told that an Arab presence would improve *their* economic lot?

Arab argumentation was not better. Taking a leaf from confused Zionist claims, they stressed that Jews had come to Palestine because of antisemitic persecution in Europe. So why did the poor Palestinians have to pay for something they had not done? I tried to explain that antisemitism was only one of the components in the whole complex of Zionist thought. Jew-hatred and persecutions actually led far more Jews to America than to Palestine. I pointed out that the driving component of the Zionist idea was the Yearning-for-Zion element, the historical attachment of the people of Israel to the Land of Israel. Whether they liked it or not, Arabs were doing themselves a disservice by not recognizing what Zionism was really about: the deep attachment of the Jewish people to their ancestral country, a belief rooted in Jewish consciousness that Israel is part of the Jewish historical identity. My argument made little headway. Of course, to accept it would have weakened the Arabs' case very much.

The effort to find a path through the maze of Arab and Israeli arguments and counter-arguments was complicated by the fact that there were too many fanatics in both camps. Fanatics who claimed that the Land was all ours—or theirs—because God had decided so or because destiny—or natural right, or history—had decreed it. In such a level of discourse, even relatively sober people lost their wits. Wishful thinking became king. There was the colorful, charismatic, but not always responsible Moshe Dayan, proclaiming in the early 1970s that never had the security situation of Israel been better—until the Yom Kippur War of 1973 erupted. Or Itzhak Rabin, our Defense Minister about fifteen years later—and a very responsible type— declaring at the start of the *intifada* that this was only a local unrest that would be easily quelled. Or stupidest of all, those Arabs who dreamed about the "conquest of Jerusalem" and the destruction of the "Zionist entity" and actually prepared themselves for it.

Decades of military tension and propaganda resulted in a grim ideological harvest. In spite of a generation of conflict, no deep-rooted hatred against the Arabs developed among most Israelis. The same could not be said about the Arabs. Decades of propaganda among the poorly educated masses of the Arab countries brought about a worrying demonization of Jews and Israelis (no distinction was made between them) in popular Arab consciousness. The propaganda sounded very similar to the worst notions of Jews that were so common (and sometimes still are) in Europe. By the 1980s, ideological argumentation and fantasy had become one of the major obstacles in the way of an understanding between Jews and Arabs.

There was one moment in the history of the conflict when a solution was at hand: in 1947, when the United Nations reached its decision about the partition of Palestine between Jews and Arabs. While it is true that by 1947 the situation in Palestine was already ideologically burdened by the ongoing conflict, the partition represented a great opportunity to close one chapter and open a new and better one, and to do so in the context of an international decision and under international auspices. The Jews accepted it. The Arabs chose the path of war.

It was a mistake of colossal proportions. Historically considered, confrontation worked to Israel's advantage. The Jews were stronger, or perhaps more modern, or more resolute. The Arabs were disunited, starry-eyed, intolerant not only of the Jews but also of Arab factions other than their own. Half a century later, it no longer mattered within what frontiers a "definitive" Israel would exist, or if the Palestinians would or would not establish an independent state. Arab Palestine would still be highly dependent on Israel for vital elements of his existence. The Arabs had erred. History is no welfare institution: In history, if one errs, one pays.

In the meantime, the confrontation became a full-fledged international problem, involving the whole Middle East and drawing into it countries beyond the region. The conflict remained a dominant political issue in every Middle Eastern country. It continued to cause much misery, endless internal and external problems, a staggering squandering of resources which Israel, at least, could hardly afford. There was the danger of worse things to come—and how would it end?

The Arab-Israeli confrontation is the only issue in my experience where my intellectual tools seemed to lure me to the side of the extremists. I found it difficult to argue about the conflict with a sober Israeli, one who actually shared my fears and hopes—honestly so—yet did not believe a solution was feasible. "Evyatar, don't be naive!" I would be told. "How can you expect Arabs, in this era of their national renaissance and pride, to accept that Zionist thorn in the very heart of the Arab nation? Don't you see that the whole debate about peace in the Middle East is more a discussion between Jew and Jew, than between Jew and Arab? Evyatar, you are a historian. When in history did a people [meaning, the Arabs] give up freely what they were convinced belonged to them? Of course, the Arabs are human beings as we, with the same fears and hopes. It is not that they lack good will, or would not like peace as much as we do. It is simply that one cannot ask another society to give up something that is not in its power to bestow. They simply are unable to accept our political existence. The conflict is unavoidable."

Indeed, I pondered, is it not so? Who is there to talk to? Could I ignore the fate of those Arab activists and leaders who had spoken for peace with Israel and had been assassinated—indeed, did any of them remain alive? And what about those very wise Jews in the past, who, driven by moderation, or by what they considered political insight, proposed a variety of political compromises? There were no sustained, successful negotiations between moderates on both sides—and it is unlikely that the modern Jewish state would have emerged from any such negotiations.

Yet I find some reasons to hope. There are very convincing indications that by the 1990s the era of confrontation has lost its meaning for both sides. Not because Arabs and Israelis have become that peaceful (they have not), but because there remains very little advantage to be gained by either side, by whatever violent means. The disproportion between what is to be gained and what could be lost has become such that political compromises are imperative, for both sides. In the realities of the 1990s, much can be destroyed, little can be changed. But how long will it take for all the participants in the Middle Eastern equation to recognize this and to sit down and work out—honestly—a political solution? Until then, we all must hold on, and pray that no major disaster occurs.

&

Religion in Israel, meaning its political and public aspects, is another theme I have reflected on—and debated and worried about—for many years. I am a non-religious Jew, which obviously has influenced my view of the issue. Historical work has taught me the centrality of the religious factor in Jewish historical identity. In general, I think it is desirable that religious custom has influenced the formation of modern Israeli society. Of course, religious ways are very much a part of life in Jerusalem. Yet it has always surprised me to discover how many people keep Jewish rites and customs, or at least some of them, in Israeli communities that are more strongly influenced by secular trends than Jerusalem. With regard to Diaspora Jewry, I doubt today that non-observant Jews there will manage to avoid total assimilation into the Gentile environment.

It was not religion as such that worried me, but the politicization of religion, as well as that very modern issue, the relation between religion and state. To say that it is an exceedingly complex matter would be a banality. In Western Europe, the church-state question has been intricate and difficult. In Muslim countries, where religious fundamentalism is on the rise, the issue has become truly explosive. Its consequences may also be dangerous for us.

In Israel, a large sector of the religious or tradition-minded population have accepted explicitly or implicitly the principle of separation between politics and religion. Many of these people belong to or vote for one of the secular parties. There has always been a small group of Jews connected either with the religious Reform or the religious Conservative movements. Although in the United States these religionists comprise an overwhelming majority of the Jewish population, in Israel they constitute a tiny minority, permanently abused by the Orthodox majority.

About fifteen percent of the Israeli population regularly votes for parties that espouse religious Orthodoxy. They represent a point of view about the rights and the position of religion to which I am totally opposed. For me and many others, the claim by religious politicians that in a Jewish state matters of general policy cannot be separated from matters of religious creed is as hollow and self-serving in Israel as it ever was in Europe. We understand that nowhere has a religious establishment adapted to progress easily, or peacefully. Conservatism, even reactionaryism seems an essential element in the character of organized religion, in Israel as anywhere else.

In the 1980s, an irksome mess developed. During this period, the strength of the two larger political parties, Likud and Labor, was fairly evenly balanced. The religious parties became indispensable partners in governmental coalitions, despite their relatively small size. Worse, each segment of Israeli Orthodoxy became politicized, and they were supported by Diaspora Jews with similar views. Orthodoxy was divided into a Sephardic and an Ashkenazic branch. Part of the Ashkenazic faction, although participating in most government-sponsored activities and extremely keen on governmental budgets, had not yet officially recognized the State of Israel—after all, the Messiah had not yet arrived. Some of these Ashkenazi refuse to serve in the army under one pretext or another, a sore point in relations between secular and religious Israelis. This Ashkenazic faction was further divided into *Hasidic* and anti-*Hasidic* sub-branches, which hated each other with astonishing fierceness. There was also a religious-Zionist party, which not only produced some of the most daring soldiers of the army, but was one of the spearheads of the Greater Israel movement (all of the Land is God-given to the Jewish people).

Visitors frequently asked me why we accepted such a situation. There was an easy answer: we ourselves were responsible for it; the religious parties were acting according to the strict rules of democratic politics, as they exist in Israel. But there is another, deeper reason. If you scratch the surface of a non-religious Israeli, not far beneath you will find an Orthodox Jew. How far are we from them? One, two generations? I myself, the non-believer, am more at home in an Orthodox than in a Reform synagogue. In fact, I feel very comfortable there. Memories of bygone days are stirred, from my childhood, sitting with my father in the *shul* (synagogue), the familiar smell of his prayer shawl in which I used to bury my face, the sing-song of the cantor, the response of the congregation. . . .

Perhaps I and people like me do not always take the extreme Orthodox seriously enough. There is something folkloric about those people clad in black, walking in the scorching heat of the October holy days under thick *shtraimels* (fur hats), proper head-gear for the Russian winters of long ago. They tried to live in the eighteenth century, thundering against radio, against television, against pants-dressed women. Such an attitude could not be serious, we thought, it could not be sustained, it was a tempo-rary aberration. Individually considered, many of these Ortho-dox were beautiful people, clean souls, men and women of great honesty. And there was so much Jewish strength in them! It was only a matter of time, they would eventually awaken. Though sometimes they were rather ridiculous. For instance, at a public demonstration of the extreme Orthodox that ninety-year-old rab-bi, railing (half in Yiddish, half in Hebrew) against the *kibbutzim*, those bastions of the Devil. The man would not recognize a *kibbutz* if he landed in the middle of one! But was it really ridicu-lous? Ten thousand black-clad zealots filled the demonstration site, applauding wildly.

We underestimated the intelligence of our own people. The situation might indeed be temporary—but in the meantime, the extreme Orthodox were doing very well. If there is an underlying moral in politics (and I am convinced there is), we had landed in the worst of all situations: the politically religious acquired a great deal of power, with no corresponding public responsibility. They were oblivious to the principle of diverse segments of the popula-tion coexisting democratically in a modern Jewish state. They were aggressive toward and intolerant of secular Israelis, reli-gious Israelis or Jews who did not conform to strict Orthodoxy, and Orthodox Jews whose positions did not conform exactly to the whims (or was it the interests?) of this or that branch of Ortho-doxy. Since there were at least four competing religious parties, each had to "prove" itself against the others: to show which one truly served God. This religious political activity brought in its wake corruption both small and large. Sanctimonious rhetoric aside, many people believed that the religious parties' political support could be bought, one time by Labor, another by Likud. The only question was, who would make the higher bid.

Political power bred political appendage: gradually a clerical establishment of truly Middle Eastern proportions arose in Israel, comprising religious politicians, functionaries, inspectors and activists, all of whom lived on public sinecures. Early in the 1980s, my father asked me to pursue a matter for him in the Ministry of Religions ("religion*s*," since in principle there was more than one religion in Israel). My parents were then living with my sister Edith in Kibbutz Bror Hail. Bror Hail had a synagogue, and my father, who was moderately religious, took care of it. The synagogue was in need of repairs, and he had written to the ministry to get some help. Since no answer had come, he asked me to find out what had happened.

I went to the Ministry of Religions. There were the typical long corridors of governmental offices, rooms on each side, on each door the name of the official responsible for a department, or a sub-department—and nobody within! At the end of a second corridor I found a room, and there sat Rabbi X, the assistant-director of the sub-sub-department in charge of some rather mysterious field of religious enterprise. Rabbi X was deeply immersed in a huge Talmud folio that occupied half of his desk. Cautiously I stated my business. He raised his eyes, looked at me, remained silent for a moment, shook his head, returned to his Talmud. I tried to fathom what this meant. He was not the right person to address? He did not know? He did not understand? No: he did not care! Rabbi X had much more important matters to ponder. I soon learned how to do business with the Ministry of Religions: one spoke with the clerical workers. Those worthy women had business firmly in hand and settled matters without disturbing their bosses.

How did religious Orthodoxy become entrenched in Israel's political system? The first seeds were planted at the beginning of this century, when a debate arose between the non-religious and the religious Zionists regarding cultural activity within the framework of the Zionist movement. The religious opposed such activities vehemently, fearing that it would weaken religious traditions and principles. Theodor Herzl, the leader of the movement, decided to avoid the issue. Given the prevailing conditions, it was a prudent attitude. Herzl was well aware of the destructive potential inherent in any confrontation on matters of religion. He had seen France, just emerging from the Dreyfus Affair, almost torn apart by a crisis in which church-state relations played a major role. Why force the issue now, in the young and not yet stable Zionist movement? From the point of view of an early twentieth-century European liberal, religion seemed in retreat. If this was so, why inflate an issue that time would solve?

For decades, that line of thought was conventional wisdom in the Zionist movement. It seems that both the religious branch of the Zionist movement and the non-Zionist Orthodox segment of the Jewish population in Palestine implicitly accepted the secular prognosis about the retreat of religion. Their political behavior was defensive, aimed at protecting their endangered walls against the onslaught of non-believers. The socialist leadership, which had dominated the Zionist movement and the Jewish community in Palestine for decades, considered organized religion an irritant, but one they could live with. Among the problems facing the Jewish people and the Zionist movement in mid-century, one demand or another from a couple of rabbis hardly seemed important.

The leadership should have known better. Tensions and troubles, some lasting for decades, will afflict any society that has not worked out a modus vivendi between its secular and religious citizens. There was no reason to hope that Jewish society could avoid the issue. Ignored now, the question would only arise with doubled intensity later. In Palestine there was one moment when a satisfying relationship between the sides could have been worked out: when the Jewish state was created in 1948. But the opportunity was wasted. There had been no redefinition between religious and political functions in the new state.

Despite the predictions, Jewish religion had not disappeared in Israel. Why should it have? On the contrary, it thrived in the favorable climate of a state and society which were Jewish. And the decline of secular social theories and hopes gave religion an additional boost. The political structure of Israel, which in fact stimulated the political organization of the religious and their thrust for political power, had done the rest.

In the 1980s, the issue of politicized religion in Israel defied the wisdom of everyone. I disagreed with many of my acquaintances, who considered the extreme Orthodox, the "blacks," to be the main problem. I still believed that their present influence was a temporary phenomenon and would hold only until a wiser electoral system reduced them to their appropriate public dimensions. As I saw it, the extreme Orthodox rejection of modernity created such a gap between them and Israeli society at large that their influence was severely limited. Time would force them to change, to adapt, to modernize. If not, they would end closeted among themselves, dreaming about a world that even within the narrow walls of their neighborhoods was artificial.

However, there was one segment among the religious that truly worried me: those fanatics who believed that the Jewish people had reached the Messianic age, meaning the time when the old Jewish commonwealth should be reestablished, the Temple in Jerusalem rebuilt, a theocracy imposed. Theirs was a kind of modernization I was highly suspicious of, because it touched external forms and left inner concepts untouched. On that most basic of modern political issues—democracy versus religious principle—their positions were clear-cut: God came first. The state, especially a Jewish state, was made to serve God—to serve Him as they understood service. In unholy alliance with right-wing secular nationalists, religious extremists learned how to manipulate all the instrumentalities of the state—political representation, legal action, and so on—but they would only continue to participate in the political process so long as the state served their own ends.

It may sound inconsistent, but I found myself resigned to the politicization of religion in Israel. To hope, in the face of prevailing Israeli conditions, for the non-politicization of the religious forces seemed to me little more than wishful thinking. After all, it was the business of the religious to choose their own ways of public activity in the country. The crux of the matter was to guarantee the essence of democratic coexistence. I accepted a situation where various elements in the political equation—diverse religious trends, diverse non-religions positions—could "interact": meaning, could strive according to democratic principle for their rights and views. Political Israel could not be copied from any other country. It had to be created from the inside of Israeli society, yet it was clear that this would be a long and difficult road for everybody.

One point I thought was important is the principle of religious pluralism. Considered worldwide, the majority of religious Jews do not belong to the Orthodox branch. In Israel the Orthodox are the majority among the religious, but even here there are many religious Jews who are not, or not exactly, Orthodox. They, and their synagogues and organizations, have their right to exist and to act publicly. This was the case of the Progressives, associated with the Reform and Conservative movements in American Jewry. But the Progressives seemed to illuminate the problems of modern Jewish religion from an additional angle. How was it that in the United States they encompassed a majority of American Jews, while in Israel they were an insignificant minority? How to explain the astonishing fact that in Israel, where the overwhelming majority of the population were non-Orthodox Jews, the Progressives had made very little headway? I was convinced it was their own fault. Even though by the 1990s there were quite a number of native-born Israelis among their rabbis, they simply did not know how to relate to Israelis. This impression was strengthened by recurring discussions I had with leaders of the Reform and the Conservative movements, in Israel and in the United States, about their views of Israeli public life. These conversations would usually develop like a chess game. The opening play was our agreement that the religious Progressive movement was discriminated against and ridiculed by the Orthodox establishment. Then I made the next move:

"Say, why don't you people form a political party and run some candidates in the next Israeli elections?"

"We? Never! [deep indignation]. It is against our principles! We are a religious movement, not a political party!"

"But look, every unworldly hasidic rebbe in Mea Shearim" [the most Orthodox neighborhood in Jerusalem]—"nay, every unworldly hasidic rebbe in Brooklyn!—understood long ago that the way to acquire influence, power and funds in Israel is to turn political. And here you are, modern, sophisticated, political-minded about every nuance of life—how come you behave so clumsily when it comes to Israeli politics?"

At that point, slightly disturbed expressions would pass over my interlocutors' faces. But they recovered quickly:

"But we are too few! We would never manage to elect a Knesset member!"

I avoided bringing up the rather nasty question that nagged me. What were these people actually afraid of? Of losing or winning that theoretical election? To avoid embarrassment, I would say:

"*I* would vote for your political slate. I am non-religious, but the principle of religious pluralism in Israel is highly important for me. And like me, many others would vote for you too."

Nevertheless, these conversations always left uneasy feelings. I wondered to what degree my colloquists' hearts and minds were engaged in Israeli life—whether they were still more at home in the United States—and they knew that I wondered. Obviously we Israelis still have a considerable way to go on the issue of religion in Israel, on the matter of coexistence between the religious and non-religious factions among our population and even between the religious factions themselves.

◌

For me, does all this add up to some integrated view about Israel? Or, as I sometimes am asked, am I a Zionist? I certainly consider myself one, although among the ideological thinkers in modern Judaism I feel closer to Simon Dubnow, the father of Jewish Autonomism, than to Theodore Herzl, the founder of political Zionism, or even to Ahad Haam, the great exponent of cultural Zionism. I definitely feel estranged from a Zionism that writes off the Diaspora, yet at the same time, I believe that Jewish life in Israel is much fuller, more creative, with deeper potential, than in *Galut*, in the Diaspora. I do not know if it is more secure. Perhaps Jews in the United States are more secure than we here, in the volatile Middle East. But does it really matter? Collective danger is as much a part of life as collective security.

I care little about the approach that emphazises the "Zionist revolution," or the belief that Zionism started Jewry anew, or the view that Israel should produce a new edition of the Hebrew of old. This is why I find the Israeli custom of changing one's name to "hebraize" it something definitely quaint. As I have said, I did myself change my first name—from Siegfried to Evyatar—but I have regretted it ever since. I also considered changing my family name, but my father—be his memory blessed!—managed to convince me to wait a bit, then another bit, then another, until I came to my senses.

Israel, as I see it, is not the end of Jewish history, but only a link in the continuing chain of Jewish life. It may well be that in another century new political and social concepts will make the state obsolete. We seem to witness the first signs of such a development in Europe, though not yet in the Middle East, where all the advantages and disadvantages of aggressive statehood are still being experienced.

I would call myself a post-Zionist. The existence of a Jewish state seems to me essential, but for reasons that have to do not with antisemitism, or the Holocaust, but with modernity. In the social and political conditions of modern Western society, I believe that Jewish statehood is the right way to guarantee the continuing existence of the Jewish people. More than solving all the problems of Jewish life, Israel seems to express many of them, but it does so in the terms and realities of our contemporary world.

∾

In what direction is Israeli society moving? After nearly a half-century, Israel has emerged as surprisingly stable politically, especially in light of its many problems. The balance between the main political forces has remained unchanged for more than a generation. In the elections of 1977, a major political upheaval had occurred: the center-right Likud party wrested political control from the center-left Labor party. Likud has been in power since then. As is usual in the Israeli political tradition, the significance of the 1977 shift was obscured by the din of high-sounding slogans. But all this was mainly pretense. In effect, the new Israeli middle class had come into power. The Likud party retained its role in government because new Israelis hoped to enjoy the good life that people were experiencing in America and in Europe. And if the Israeli economy could not afford this, then—are we Jews not the wizards of finance?—let us simply print the money to underwrite the new life! Six years later the orgy was over, the country sunk in financial disaster.

My own awakening came somewhere in the middle of this period, during a conversation with a Jerusalemite Arab about the chances of peace in the Middle East now that the Likud party, some of whose leaders were raving extremists, was in power. "What is the difference?" he remarked. "Aren't you all Zionists?" Indeed we were, and this view from the outside helped me gain a better perspective on matters. If our political differences were less significant to others than they were to us, what had happened? Israel had become "normal"—that is, normal up to a point. In a country surrounded by enemies, suffering from the effects of an economic boycott, a human patchwork of immigrants still searching for a new collective identity, not much normalcy could be expected.

The 1977 political upheaval, which was consolidated in 1981, was the inevitable outcome of a gradual process. Decades of socialist government had led to the corrosion of values and corruption that too much time in power always seems to breed. A new sector of the population, the immigrants of the 1950s and their children—many of them from Muslim countries—found very little meaning in the axioms of the old leadership. The 1973 Yom Kippur War and its aftermath further undermined the prestige of the ruling caste. The politicians had ruthlessly shoved responsibility for their own blunders onto the shoulders of the army commanders. In the end the voters chose a leadership closer, not so much to their ideals, but to their interests.

Those middle-class interests usually cause discomfort to the intellectual, particularly since he shares them but is rather ashamed of it. But the new Israeli middle class, now proudly rearing its head, was downright embarrassing. Without the redeeming charm of some common cultural tradition, without the softening influence of established manners and a sensitivity for good form, the behavior of those Israeli burghers and their raw acquisitiveness seemed uncouth and disgusting. The aggressiveness of the new Israelis mortified me. At bottom, it was more characteristic of a society of immigrants. Among themselves, in the context of their many "ethnic" groups—which had established codes of conduct—Israelis knew very well how to behave. But in the broader Israeli society, where the barriers of old traditions did not function well, the lowest common denominator of behavior imposed itself. Whatever the explanation for their behavior, it was hard to take. I was always astonished when foreigners found charm in the lack of formality, in the so-called "naturalness" of the Israeli. I thought it was insupportable.

Yet I was wrong. No society lives only on interests. There are always values operating beneath the surface, giving some general direction to life. My foreign visitors showed more sensitivity, or perhaps greater empathy, for the tacit qualities of Israeli life. Like these foreigners, Israelis, too, wanted new cars and the other goodies of modern life. But the visitors also perceived qualities and virtues in my fellow Israelis that I, in my scorn, preferred to ignore. They sensed powerful undercurrents in Israeli society, which sometimes seemed greater and worthier than the people who presently embodied them: the great dream of the Redemption, deeply imbued, in one form or another, in all walks of Israeli life; the undertones of the Catastrophe, the Holocaust, pulsating somberly in Israeli consciousness; the fear of mothers and wives when sons and husbands were called to the army, still, again, one generation later, two generations later; the burdens and joys of a great religious faith.

In the meantime, however, how did one live in such a country? How did one deal with all these tensions? Strangely enough, in spite of all the problems and difficulties, Israel teemed with vitality, with the will and ability to live. In the 1980s, while working on the statistics of my *Atlas of Modern Jewish History*, I came upon a fact: the median age of the Jewish population in Israel was astonishingly low—26.8 years in 1980. If we consider Israel a Western country—which I think it is, even if a rather peculiar one—this was the lowest median age in the Western world at that time. In modern societies the number of children per family has typically decreased. Yet in Israel it had remained relatively high and stable, was even increasing. In the 1980s the typical Israeli Jewish family had approximately three children. Among religious Jews, the number was generally higher than that. The best explanation I could offer is that the Jewish population of Israel is basically an optimistic one, convinced that despite everything, it can cope with the problems of the present, and cope successfully. Israel is onwards-directed, hopeful about its future.

"Sir, what kind of state is Israel?" I was once asked after a lecture in Atlanta. My answer, more from my heart than from my head, was:

"Israel is a state of mind."

19

First Visits to the United States

The fact that my first days in America were spent outside a metropolis helped me, I believe, gain a balanced view of the United States. I have known many people whose first impressions of America were formed by New York, or Washington, or Boston. My first American week, in the summer of 1970, was spent in Louisville, Kentucky. I worked there in the Brandeis Archives, in the Law School library of the University of Louisville. From there I took a Greyhound bus to Cincinnati, Ohio, to the American Jewish Archives, where I spent several weeks.

The natural efficiency of the American style of life and the natural cordiality of Midwestern people made a lasting impression on me. This was strengthened later when my family and I spent a year in Columbus, Ohio. My subjective feeling about America is that the United States is somehow centered on the Midwest, is anchored there, draws from this region its sense of life and proportion. However, from the start I never suffered from the common misconception: that I knew America, or Americans. Few countries are as varied as the United States.

Among Americans (or non-Americans) of self-declared sophistication, Louisville, Cincinnati, and Columbus are not considered, let us say, the most exciting places in the world. Yet I have returned there again and again, especially to Upper Arlington, the neighborhood in which we lived in Columbus. Upper Arlington retains for me a dream-like quality. There is something hardly real about that place, those upper-middle-class houses among all the trees, the green lawns, the beautiful gardens, here and there a brook, and an overall quality of spaciousness that is more and more difficult to find anywhere.

American friendships born in those years, from 1970 to 1976, have continued throughout my life, and this seems to be part of the positiveness of my first American experiences. At the Hebrew Union College I met Jacob R. Marcus, one of the senior historians of American Jewry, courtly in a Southern way and extremely friendly. In 1970 Marcus was already over seventy. Almost twenty years later, during another visit to Cincinnati, Marcus, still well and active, introduced me, the lecturer of almost sixty, as "my boy. . . ." Another lifelong friendship that began in Cincinnati was with Stan Chyet, the kindest of men. Later I met Marc Raphael, who paved the way for us during my first stay with my family in Columbus, and to whom I owe many insights into American Jewish academic life. And Carol and Jeff Folkerth, who became an essential part of my Upper Arlington experience.

During my M.A. studies I had become interested in American and American Jewish history. My first scholarly book was on the development of American Zionism in the years 1898–1914. The main lesson I learned from my research for that book was that Zionism in the United States was radically different from the European model. Historical attachment of the Jewish people to the Land of Israel is a major factor in Zionism, a complex factor in Jewish self-definition that Gentiles (and sometimes Jews, too) find difficult to understand. Together with the frustrations of the Jewish experience in modern Europe, this attachment resulted in the quest—powerfully embodied in the Zionist movement—to rebuild the Jewish homeland in Palestine. However, Jewish disillusion with modern conditions was a European phenomenon. America was different, and American Zionism had some original, albeit confusing characteristics. In American

Zionism there was a strong tendency to become part of the developing American Jewish community. Although committed to the creation of a Jewish home in Palestine, American Zionists strove to participate in the strengthening of the institutions of American Jewry. That seeming contradiction in goals did not lead to confusion and aimlessness. Rather it seemed to instill into the American Zionist leadership a clarity of vision and a purposefulness greater than that found in many other segments of American Jewry. This phenomenon was and remains an inexplicable riddle for the European Zionist activists who have visited the United States and written about Zionism there. None of them has understood that the motto "Zionism plus Diaspora, Palestine plus America"—formulated by Israel Friedlaender in the early twentieth century—was not an ideological deviation, but an expression of the facts of Jewish life in America and, as such, worthy of recognition and acceptance.

Strangely enough, American Jewry was a theme that hardly interested my colleagues and teachers, despite the fact that by the mid-twentieth century almost half of the world's Jewish population was living in the U.S. In 1959, Moshe Davis came to the Hebrew University to teach American Jewish history. I attended one of his seminars, but we never got close. Among my colleagues, I was for years the only non-American working on American Jewish history. The theme was not popular with students, either: a course on German Jewry would fill a classroom; a course on American Jewry would attract only half-a-dozen students, mostly American immigrants. Only in the 1980s did that situation change.

In 1968 I met Ben Halpern, who visited Israel periodically. His book *The Idea of the Jewish State* was, at the time, one of the few academic works in its field. I knew also his ideas about the development of American Jewry and about Zionism in the U.S. Our meeting was extremely cordial, the first step in a relationship that would continue for many years. Halpern was tall, somewhat shy. He showed genuine interest in what I was doing. He stimulated me to continue my work and suggested that I visit the United States. I went away with the clear feeling that Halpern represented another human type in my experience. It would take time and better knowledge about American society to "localize" him. Despite his genuine Jewishness and his commitment to Jewish causes and Jewish history, Halpern was also the embodiment of a New England Yankee gentleman. And in contrast to many American Jews I came to know later, his behavior was totally unaffected.

Nowhere did I feel my "israeliness" more than when meeting with American Jews. Not because I was that different: on the contrary. After all, I had grown up in Brazil, a Diaspora country. But in the company of American Jews I became aware of the changes that my years in Israel had brought about in me.

Most American Jews I came in contact with had inconsistent perspectives on Jewish issues, as opposed to American ones. As American intellectuals—professionals, men of action or thinkers—they were supremely serious and very impressive. Many of the finest analyses of American political and social situations have been done by scholars who were Jews. Jews were among the most representative and trusted figures in American life. However, when it came to judging Jewish affairs, their performance seemed to me shallower, much less convincing. Perhaps this was because American Jewry was still young: after all, the present community was founded less than 150 years ago. Or perhaps it had to do with the realities of living as a minority, in the conditions of the modern Western world. Whatever the reason, I found the lack of harmony between their general and their Jewish perspectives disturbing, and I tried to understand it.

The reaction of American Jewish interlocutors to my observations was frequently sharp: "You Israelis, how can you criticize! Look at yourself: what confusion reigns in your public life! How many political parties were there, at your last elections? Fifteen? What exactly, would you please explain, are the differences between them, especially between 'your' religious parties? Incidentally, they are all Orthodox, aren't they? And talking about religion, when are you going to emerge from the Middle Ages? You know, there is something called separation between state and religion in modern society!"

The observation had truth to it, but the point seemed irrelevant to me. Contemporary Jews are all struggling with the problem of Jewish identity. It seems inevitable that this struggle would take on diverse forms in Israel and in the Jewish Diaspora, and that these diversities would frequently be at odds with each other. It was a quarrel between brothers; we knew how much we had in common, but there were differences in approach. And when friction arose between those American Jewish colleagues and me—the Israeli who claimed to know a thing or two about American Jewish history—sparks flew. Indeed, of all the themes I have researched and written about, none led me into greater personal difficulties than when I expressed an opinion about some issue in American Jewish history or life. Hardly anyone gave me the benefit of academic doubt: my interlocutors knew in advance that my approach was "palestinocentric," or "zioncentric," or this-and-that-centric, and anyhow, who was I to understand the subtleties of the American Jewish historical process? Was it not obvious that I was principally interested in convincing American Jews (or, God forbid, their children) that the only right decision was to make *aliyah* to Israel? I learned to take all this patiently. Yet I could not stand the subtle or not-so-subtle kind of self-satisfaction displayed by many of my Jewish interlocutors. In the 1970s and 1980s, American Jewry had taken stock of its situation and come to feel satisfied with itself, as had God after the sixth day of Creation.

However, my quarrels with American Jewish colleagues had a special flavor. We clashed, but underneath there was always the knowledge that something connected us, that mysterious "Jewish peoplehood" we were aware of but had trouble defining. This did not make our disputes any easier. Quite the contrary. We Israelis are an aggressive bunch, and our rudeness is something I always feel truly embarrassed about. But some of those American Jews! Outwardly, they would seem the classical type of the middle-aged American professor: dressed in conservative gray, a short graying beard, a comfortable paunch, glasses to whose choice much attention had been paid, as it had to his whole external appearance: the serious mien, the expensive suit, the well modulated voice, the "Yankee" style. We would get along well—that is, until one ventured to express a difference of opinion. Then suddenly the whole façade collapsed, and an elderly edition of the original Brooklyn kid would jump out, fighting again some long-remembered street-corner tussle.

This belligerence would never happen with Ben Halpern, or someone like him, such as his disciple and later colleague, Jehuda Reinharz. Despite differences in age and temperament, Reinharz and I became very close friends and collaborated on diverse projects. Our academic interests were curiously complementary. I had started out working on Zionist history and written my dissertation on Chaim Weizmann. Reinharz's was on German Jewish history. Later, we switched: in the 1980s and 1990s Reinharz was writing an important biography of Weizmann, and I turned to

German Jewish history. Reinharz is a peculiar example of double Jewish identity: In Jerusalem everyone takes him for an Israeli; in the States, where he and his family live, he seems an ordinary American.

But how many Halperns and Reinharzs are there, so well attuned to Jewish life in the States *and* in Israel? I encountered some, but unfortunately they were too few. Too often I found myself being taught lessons by my American colleagues—not only about American Jewish issues, but also about Israeli matters.

Typical, on that account, was an encounter I had in Jerusalem with Irving Howe, I think it was in 1976. I had enormous respect for Howe's *World of Our Fathers,* which I considered one of the best works written on American Jewry. A mutual friend arranged for us to meet. We met, but failed to make contact; either Howe was tired, or he had little interest in the conversation. At any rate, after some minutes he fell into a monologue about the political situation in Israel. His very superficial knowledge of the topic and the country was in inverse proportion to the surety of his opinions, and nothing that I could say made any difference. As with many American Jewish intellectuals, he was emotionally committed to the existence of the Jewish state, but rather arrogantly so: he knew more about its problems than Israelis did, and had no difficulty saying so.

A somewhat different tack, but a not dissimilar frame of mind, I found later in Saul Bellow's *To Jerusalem and Back.* As with Howe, for Bellow everything in Israel posed a problem, usually a vital one. That there are also unproblematic dimensions to Israeli life, that Israelis love to eat and drink together, that they laugh a lot and have a fabulous sense of humor—these facets apparently escaped Bellow and Howe altogether. They had little sense of the achievements of Israeli society. The very fact that there *is* something like an Israeli society, growing slowly out of the meeting of immigrants from dozens of diverse countries and cultures; the flexibility of Israeli democracy, under so much internal and external pressure but yet functioning quite well; the strong structure of the Israeli family; and finally, the essential optimism of the Israeli, ever complaining and never satisfied, yet always hoping and trying for something better—all this went unperceived.

Only after years of contact with American Jewish writers and scholars did I come to understand how much their lives as American intellectuals and their training as political activists conditioned their reactions to Israel and its issues. They were specialists in ideological warfare, with limited sensibility to all other dimensions of life. Their battles had been fought in the American arena. Now they aimed (occasionally) their powerful intellectual guns at the Israeli scene. Both Bellow and Howe looked upon Israel as an ideological battlefield, which indeed it was, but hardly in the way they understood it.

20

Between American and Israeli Jews

       Despite my criticism of certain American Jews, I came to understand that there are issues in modern Jewish life and consciousness where we Israelis could learn a lesson or two from Jews in the United States. Most of my American interlocutors agreed that there were, indeed, areas where American Jewry could profit from contact with Israel—with its undiluted Jewishness, its Jewish vitality and the concentration of Jewish life and culture in the country. Strangely enough, I frequently found myself having to convince my American Jewish friends that *they* had much to offer us, or that their achievements in general could be instructive to us.

      American Jewry has reached a level of integration into American life that, whatever its price and problems, is greater than any such integration attained in Europe. This is a crucial point for gaining insight into American Jewish life, but one that most of us Israelis fail to grasp properly. We see American Jews chiefly as Jews, and cannot, or will not understand that they are no less (and in many cases, much more) Americans. In general, most of us Israelis have a single focus on contemporary Jewish life; we do not view it through the lens of someone who belongs to two worlds, Jewish and Gentile. This is an understandable result of our own existential condition, but one which, in my opinion, hardly makes us any wiser.

The ability to be both a Jew and an American, I came to recognize, is one of the great achievements of American Judaism. It is quite a complex position. With the exception of some fringe phenomena, every significant segment of American Judaism presents its own combination of Jewish and American components, sometimes tending more to the Jewish, sometimes more to the American side. But whatever balance is struck, both elements are integrated. A very Orthodox American rabbi is, nevertheless, very American as well. Indeed, I believe that American Jews are more American than German Jews ever became German. They belong to the mainstream of life in the United States to a degree that German Jewry has never managed to reach in Germany.

True, one of the main factors allowing such an evolution to occur is the openness of American society. So what? If American society is so open, Jews might simply have assimilated and disappeared as Jews, as indeed had happened (and was happening) to many of them. However, they developed an impressive structure of Jewish life, with its own patterns of religious belief, and they were flexible and imaginative in fostering the growth of their organizational activities. What we have been witnessing in the United States is one of the great creations of modern Jewish life, and it deserves to be recognized as such. At the same time, one can still be aware of the many troubling questions rooted in the situation of American Jewry.

Furthermore, American Jewry has reached an envious position with regard to that most delicate issue in modern Jewish life, the question of society and religion. They are a model of how the separation between religion and state need not harm Judaism in any way, and how religious pluralism is possible in modern society. I am aware that much of Jewish religious life in the United States lacks that essential condition of religious belief: fervor. But it is much better adapted to the imperatives of modern life than the variety developing in Israel, which in my opinion seems to be turning the social and political structure of Israeli society backwards.

That is not what most of my Israeli interlocutors thought,

however. They took most of my opinions with more than a grain of salt. Predictably, they argued that some of the accomplishments of American Jewry are only the inevitable outcome of a Jewish society established in the midst of Gentiles. Other achievements, such as the separation between church and state, are actually characteristic of American society in general, naturally adopted by the Jews. One can hardly consider them accomplishments of American Jewry as such. Even if they are, it was argued, there is little to be learned for Israeli purposes: it is doubtful that they could be adapted to the completely different situation of Jews living in a Jewish state. And finally, if American Jewry really wanted to influence this or that situation in Israel, fine. But where were they? How did they intend to do it? By writing articles in *Commentary?* By publishing ads in *The New York Times?* My interlocutors pointed out that Russian Jews pouring into Israel since the late 1970s were quite unprepared for the lifestyle of Israeli society or for the structure of the Israeli political system—or, at least, they were much less prepared than American Jews were. But in the end those Russian Jews would have a greater influence on the development of Israel, whatever direction it took, than American Jewry: they, at least, were there.

My Israeli interlocutors had a point. I had my own doubts about the situation of American Jewry. My historical research has led me to conclude that the golden age of American Jewish public life and creativity was during the first two decades of the twentieth century. Indeed, I have asserted that the level of American Jewish leadership in the first half of the present century—when figures such as Jacob H. Schiff, Louis Marshall, Judah L. Magnes and others emerged—was superior to the level of American Jewish leadership in the second half.

Nevertheless, my training as a historian has taught me to be sceptical about such a critical trend of thought, even though I myself contributed to it. They were logical, my fellow Israelis, up to a point. But if there is one truth I have learned in my calling, it is the importance of being simultaneously devoted to and suspicious of logical analysis, when it is called on to explain the behavior of human society. From a logical perspective, the European world seemed fixed and stable when I arrived in Germany in September 1989. Yet within a couple of weeks everything had turned upside down.

An examination of the historical way of American Jewry demonstrates clearly how frequently logic and life are incongrous. A typical example is the attitude of American Jews toward Israel. What could be more logical than the opinion, current after the establishment of the Jewish state in 1948, that from now on Diaspora Jewry and Israeli Jewry would go their separate ways? Arthur Koestler formulated it very convincingly: Jews who wanted to help nurture the Jewish state would go to Israel. Those who did not would remain in their own countries, eventually either disappearing as Jews or else developing some new Jewish identity. Whatever the future had in store, Koestler wrote, one thing was clear: the mythical Wandering Jew had finally arrived at the end of his journey.

A not dissimilar trend of thought appeared at the same time in Israel. When I arrived in the country in 1953, it was commonly believed that the history of the Jewish people had reached a crossroads. There were those who proclaimed that Israelis would integrate—*should* integrate—into their new environment, the Middle East. They would/should (the deed was clearly father to the thought) adapt to the geography, the culture, the ways of life of the region, participate in its evolution. They would become part of it, although a rather specific part.

The notion was logical, but even then—I was still a student—I was suspicious of its proponents. Did I not hear a familiar ring in the arguments of those self-denominated New Hebrews, or Canaanites? Did it not sound like a translation into Hebrew of the same assimilationist reasonings of German or other European Jews during the nineteenth and twentieth centuries? Then the goal was to assimilate into European culture. Now it was to integrate into the Middle East, to become "normal"—but what about the historical specificity of the Jewish people and their continuing existence as such?

In any case, matters turned out differently. Forty years after the creation of the Jewish state, Jews in Israel and in the United States—as well as in other Diaspora lands—were closer than they had been in 1948. The Jewish people had not evolved in diverse, unrelated directions. The question was, how had this happened? Seeking an answer, I went in a direction where I was literally forced to recognize that there is another touchy contemporary Jewish issue on which American Jewry has had at least as much success as the Israelis: the interpretation of Zionism, its significance, in the second half of the twentieth century.

Shortly after the establishment of Israel, in the early 1950s, Ben Gurion coined a slogan that was accepted lock, stock and barrel by most sectors of Israeli society, including thinking Israelis: Zionism means *aliyah* to Israel. The corollary is that Jews who hold back, which included the majority of American Jewry, are not Zionists. Never mind that Ben Gurion was a master of ideological manipulation, always able to conjure an idea to fit a given political interest. Never mind that in classical Zionist thought there is an ideological direction highly attentive to the Diaspora, its life and development. For decades, Israelis repeated the slogan without further reflection.

In practice, however, neither the Jewish state nor Diaspora Jewry accepted the logical negative consequences of Ben Gurion's slogan. To do so would mean that each side writes the other off. In effect, this is a restatement, in not so different terms, of Koestler's prognosis. But, as I said, over the following decades relations between Israel and Diaspora Jewry grew closer. The Jewish Agency, that Zionist body completely under the control and influence of Israel, took a keen interest in Diaspora Jewry. However, among Diaspora Jews, especially in the United States, a truly significant evolution occurred, one that showed not only a practical, but also an ideological dimension. In the 1970s and 1980s, the American Jewish Reform movement, that former bastion of anti-Zionism, completed an ideological about-face that brought it into the Zionist camp. Altogether, by the 1980s it could be claimed that the vast majority of American Jewry were Zionists.

Were they? Ideologically, they often had trouble explaining themselves. But then Americans—Gentiles as well as Jews— have always had difficulty with ideological justifications, especially those couched in terms taken from the European political experience. American Jewry acted by what I came to call "ideological instinct," and in that they were right on target. The major component of the Zionist conception, the idea of the unity of the Jewish people, guided them more clearly than it had the Israelis. Their position was as much a contemporary expression of Zionism as the Israelis': As such, however, it had not only the strengths, but also all the weaknesses of Zionist thought. In particular, it revealed the classic Zionist gap between the idea and the deed, between ideological conviction and practical realization.

Reaction to my expression of such thoughts was once again sharp and negative—that is, when I dared to express them, even privately, in Israel. The critique I encountered was characterized by a measure of heat that, as always happens to me when faced with an emotional stand, I found intriguing. The more so, since the actual argumentation against my position was usually limited to a single point: if a Jew could be a Zionist without making *aliyah*, I was asked, what about the concentration of Jewish people in the Land of Israel, that central component of Zionist belief?

I faced that question as a theoretical issue: in practice, it did not matter for me if this or that proportion of the Jewish people continued living in the Diaspora. On the contrary, for reasons both subjective and objective, I feel that this is the way it should be. For instance, considering the mess we Israelis have made of several aspects of our life, it is always a soothing thought that there are still Jews in the Diaspora who might help us to do better. However, from a theoretical consideration the question is a typical example of how ideology can blind people, intelligent people, to the facts of life. The concentration of Jewish people in Israel was an historical process happening before our very eyes, but my Israeli colleagues refused to see it. In 1939, three percent of all Jews lived in Palestine. By 1950, fifteen percent were living in what had become Israel. In 1990, the figure was more than one-third. Sober demographic study indicated that by the turn of the century more than half the world's Jewish children— fifteen years of age or younger—would be living in Israel. Is it not obvious that, barring a major disaster, at some not-too-distant point in the next century the majority of Jewish people would be living in the Jewish state?

Whatever arguments Israelis and American Jews muster for their collaboration, or against it, in my opinion only one fact really matters. Eighty percent of the Jewish people live either in Israel or North America, and consequently they will decide the future of the Jewish people, whatever it may be. If the continuing existence of the Jewish people is a desirable aim, then dialogue and interaction between both groups is indispensable, whatever problems and frictions may arise. This opinion, I think, is shared by most of my American Jewish colleagues and acquaintances.

21

My Generation and Its Image

Since adolescence, autobiographies have fascinated me. I think it was Charles Morgan who wrote, in *Sparkenbroke*, that no form of literature is more difficult than autobiography. Indeed, memoir writing requires self-discipline, a firm grip on that measure of self-pity each of us has tucked away somewhere, and, what is much more subtle, control over one's intellectual self-indulgence. Obviously, one has to strike a balance between private life and social context, between nearness and distance. Last, one has to be very much aware of the peculiar subjective dimension in an autobiographical composition: actually, one's present time is the central focus; the past supplies the background material.

In 1988 I was working in the American Jewish Archives in Cincinnati, attempting to determine how diverse generations of American Jewry have influenced each other, and consequently, how a historian should divide American Jewry into generations. My principal source was the large collection of autobiographical literature, both published and unpublished, produced by American Jews. While pondering the lives of American Jewish intellectuals of the generation before my own, many of whom were still active, it dawned on me that my generation had now reached the autobiographical stage.

I found significant differences between American Jewish and European Jewish memoir writers, the latter being the group to which I and people like me were more attuned. As telling examples of the European group, examples entirely arbitrary, two important contemporary autobiographies may be mentioned: Saul Friedlaender's *When Memory Comes,* and Hans Sahl's *Exil im Exil,* written in German. Sahl's book describes the generation before Friedlaender's: those German intellectuals, Jews and non-Jews, who fled Germany in the early years of the Nazi regime. They first settled in various European countries, and later many of them moved to America. Many of those people had returned to Europe after the war, some sooner, some later. Not always to stay, but frequently for long visits. Long and painful visits. Even for those who had been successful in exile, the return to Europe forced upon them the full impact of the misspent ambiguity of their lives. That generation produced an impressive memoir literature.

Friedlaender belonged to a later group, of European Jews born in the late 1920s and in the 1930s—my own generation. Some of us had escaped Europe before the Holocaust; others, like Friedlaender himself, lived through the European inferno. In the 1970s, their voices first began to be heard, occasionally in full-fledged memoirs, but also in articles or, indirectly, through intellectual work. That generation was dispersed throughout the world. Many of its members maintained some connection with Europe, but almost none regarded a European land as his or her home-country.

Most of the German refugees of Sahl's generation spoke with a similar voice, although each one had endured a particular fate. Germany had expelled some of its most talented children, but they had not left spiritually naked: no regime could confiscate their minds. Their indignation and intellectual resistance became the rallying point for men and women everywhere against Hitler and his regime. Their autobiographical literature represented a seminal lesson for any future generation of intellectuals bent on confronting a totalitarian regime. It showed—beyond that, it imposed—an unavoidable conclusion: intellectuals, even more than politicians and certainly ahead of them, will find themselves—perhaps unwillingly—on the front line of barricades raised against dictatorship and oppression. They are, as well, always among the first victims.

By comparison, my own generation's path had been quite different. We did not begin as a culturally defined group, able to express ourselves as such. Our scholling was interrupted, to be taken up again in foreign countries and in new languages. On the surface, it seemed we were better off: we had enjoyed a regular education in the new lands where we were supposed to live—in English, in Hebrew, in Portuguese. It might appear that we had taken diverse and unrelated ways. Now that we had reached middle-age, however, it was becoming clear that we had developed something like a collective identity, although a rather strange one. We seemed to behave in peculiarly similar ways, but it would take the sharpened sensibility of one member of our generation to recognize another: we seemed to resist mutual recognition. We aimed to integrate into this or that society, not to establish our own group identity. The signs, however, were clear. One indication is a certain type of individualism which I came to recognize from afar, something that borders on arrogance. Now, the classically arrogant individual behaves this way either out of a sense of insecurity or of inflated self-assurance: he thinks (or wants to think) that he owns the world, so why not show it? The arrogance of many members of my generation has an impersonal quality. Some of the most arrogant among us are exceedingly kind persons, very generous, and with excellent manners. But they carry an aura that implies: "How do you dare to approach me? How can you understand me? What do you know?"

It could be that my impressions are tainted, because I am principally familiar with a certain stratum from my generation—people active in the professions or in universities. But most of these people have been utterly incapable of settling down: many members of my generation hold academic chairs or jobs in two universities at the same time, almost always on different continents. We dream about stability, but are unable to hold on to narrower attachments, those that give life so much of its equilibrium and meaning. We are at home everywhere—and nowhere. Highly articulate, many of the people of my generation have made a life principle out of our essential rootlessness: we are cosmopolitans, at a time when cosmopolitanism has lost much of its appeal. In fact, we remain the ultimate refugees: not because of circumstances, but as an existential condition. Nobody tries harder than we to manipulate life. Nobody has been less successful at it. We are not easy people, the members of my generation.

A recurring focus for most members of my generation is our attitude toward Israel. Israel is an issue that has divided us into two camps. I belong to the group for whom Israel, whatever its internal problems, has become home. However, I think the attitude of the other group is more typical. The adjective that describes it best is "shrill." Many members of this other group have an Israeli connection. Many have lived in Israel for longer or shorter periods, or were Israeli-educated. Some were even born in Israel: the children of refugees, they were touched by the existential disquietude of their parents or their environment and ended up leaving the country. In most cases, they owe whatever degree of psychological stability they have attained to the Israeli component in their lives. However, there are no sharper critics of Israel, its society, its culture, its way of life, its significance. To judge from the bitterness of their utterances, Israel and its people grate against a raw nerve in their psyches. They describe Israel and its society as intolerant, parochial, nationalistic, unjust. They prefer broad spiritual horizons. They are citizens of the world. They leave because in Israel it is impossible to work: Jerusalem is too confining; about Tel Aviv, the less said the better. What they need is, let us say, the spirituality of New York, the pulse of Oxford, the peacefulness of Paris. To participate in that great (if not the greatest) existential adventure of the twentieth century—Israel—for them is not enough. Obviously, the material, or social, or intellectual Israel doesn't matter. For so many of the members of my generation Jerusalem represents a psychic dimension that is the ultimate threat: a framework.

∾

Along with that well-screened internal anguish of so many members of my generation—certainly, a happy generation we are not—are there some redeeming qualities in our lives?

Shortly after my arrival in Germany in 1989, I had a conversation that gave me much to think about. It happened, of all places, on the night-train from Hamburg to Heidelberg. I had hoped to have the cramped sleeping cabin to myself. No such luck: one minute before departure a very large fellow literally crashed in—bearded, fattish, sweaty—dragging suitcases and bags, waving his ticket like a flag. We talked, and he turned out to be one of the most interesting people I met in Germany. Although he was about fifteen years younger than I, he seemed quite typical of my own generation. A physicist, born in Poland at the end of World War II, he had been educated in Sweden. From Jewish stock, but no longer a Jew. Married to a German, he was living and working somewhere between Munich and Boston with an arrangement that despite all my experience with the species I was unable to understand. And a man of truly sparkling intelligence. In that confusion, what language did we speak? We spoke English.

Why was he working in America, when his family lived in Munich? He wanted to work among Americans, who are, as he saw it, the only really creative people of our time. The French and the Germans are spiritually handicapped when it comes to scientific creation, my interlocutor asserted. The Germans are at a disadvantage because of their innate sense of hierarchy. The heads of most German scientific institutions have too much authority, they stultify younger talent. Germans are good technicians, their work is exact and reliable, but scientifically they are much too conservative. The French have a different problem. They put too much emphasis on brilliance—but brilliantly presented ideas are not necessarily original. In addition, he continued, the French are educated to think with Cartesian clarity. In itself, this is an admirable quality. Scientific creation, however, is never tidy and clear; like childbirth, it is messy and difficult. With mind and soul the creative person must try to extract from the dark and confusing mass of facts, knowledge and clashing theories some new truth, the rough diamond of a new idea, a new principle, which after much cutting and polishing would shine forth. In these days, my travel companion argued, Americans had the best conditions for scientific creation. Not all Americans, of course, but that tiny group which elevated itself over the huge mass of middle-brow American academic life. And they, they were free: unencumbered by authority, by system, by rules. They were creative.

I lay there in the dark, the train rumbling through the night, listening to him and pondering my own quest. Who more than the people of my own generation was endowed—or cursed—with that spiritual independence he was talking about? It is a characteristic I can smell from a distance: that peculiar intellectual detachment for which so heavy a price has been paid. Some members of my generation have been blessed with a freedom of mind, an ability to look at things unburdened by convention, a fresh point of view regarding humanity, society, art or knowledge that always astonishes me anew. Sometimes the price the members of my generation paid for their inner independence bordered on madness. So what? Is there really any alternative?

We were, indeed, a peculiar phenomenon. Was there some additional meaning in our condition? Or were we merely the bearers of a latter-day stigma of our Jewish fates? In the end, my reflections brought me back to a theme I had been avoiding for years: the Holocaust.

22

The Holocaust: Between Past History and Present Consequences

I was almost fifty before I did any historical work relating to the Holocaust—the essay about the non-link between the destruction of European Jewry and the creation of Israel. Even that work had a defensive character: its aim was to prove what the Holocaust was not. Later I came to realize that I had been fighting a losing battle, and I tried to understand the reasons for my original reticence. One is that I felt a deep uneasiness, almost a revulsion, over the way many Jews—both in Israel and in the Diaspora—confronted the theme. As I have already mentioned, I have something of the rebellious Hasid in me. Emotional approaches to issues turn me off sharply. And the Holocaust is too serious a theme to allow emotionalities. Yet it may happen that when the Holocaust is at issue emotions approach demagoguery. I disagreed also with the way discussion of the theme was frequently directed to some conclusion, some "lesson." I had no idea—I still have none—what the lesson of the Holocaust is supposed to be.

During a year-long stay in Germany, in 1989–90 (which I will describe shortly), several aspects related to that issue—some personal, some not—became clearer. First, I arrived at a better understanding of the degree to which the after-effects of the Holocaust are a major problem in present-day Jewish life. Second, I grasped that the Holocaust has been a major, subconscious point of reference in my historical work, even when I was dealing with themes that apparently had little to do with it. And last, I saw that my determined effort to avoid the issue was part of the problem: it was as one of the Holocaust generation that I was trying to distance myself from the Catastrophe.

∾

Probably there is no other theme in modern Jewish history, or in Jewish history in general, that has been so intensively and extensively researched and considered as the Holocaust. It seems that no major fact about the tragedy of European Jewry remains unknown, except for those—such as the absence of written orders by Hitler setting in motion the machinery of destruction—which will probably never be uncovered. Nevertheless, research continues, and frequently seems to stretch the bounds of common sense. For example, there was a symposium in Frankfurt where worthy and serious scholars debated for a long time that supposedly worthy and serious issue: whether the Holocaust had been an event of rational, irrational or anti-rational character. I have no idea what conclusions were reached, but I am ready to bet that they concluded that all three types of motivation contributed to the Holocaust. A later generation, looking with a fresh perspective at the primary sources or the accumulated literature, would likely be able to offer new insights into the topic. We, on the other hand, have apparently reached the point of saturation.

If that is so, why does a huge international research machine continue to work unabated—indeed, continue to regenerate itself? One obvious reason is that all this work is driven by an unanswered question: how could it have happened? The sobering fact is that we are as far from answers today as we were thirty years ago. An abyss still looms between knowledge and comprehension of the Catastrophe. We have more and more information; but understanding it is a different matter.

There was, however, something much more worrying: gradually I began to wonder if the after-effects of the Holocaust were not affecting me and most people I know like a cloud obscuring our understanding of our Jewish condition, as individuals and as a society. It is my deep conviction that only my training as a historian enabled me to recognize, after too long a time, our real situation.

The Catastrophe occurred at a very complex moment in modern Jewish life. Jewish society was trying to recreate that age-old equilibrium between Gentile values and influences and Jewish patterns of existence that had been an indispensable element in the continuing history of the Jewish people. Historical analysis of several indicators suggested that in the early years of the twentieth century, internal developments in Jewish society were once again leading toward such an equilibrium. The Holocaust had destroyed it, however.

Now, fifty years later, a grim picture about the consequences of the Holocaust was emerging, consequences for the Jewish Diaspora as well as for Israel. The internal weaknesses of most Diaspora communities seemed a latter-day result of the Catastrophe. Many problems related to the structure of Israeli society and its internal tensions and contradictions were, in my eyes, consequences of the Holocaust. Certainly the disappearance of old and settled Jewries, with centuries of tradition and experience behind them, left an unbridgeable void in Jewish life. But beyond this, contemporary Jewish existence appears to suffer from a kind of disorientation that seems related to the Catastrophe and becomes apparent in the ways we deal with the remembrance of the Holocaust.

These conclusions began to dawn on me several years earlier, while I was working and teaching in the United States. I have been pondering the growth of so-called "Holocaust studies" in many American universities. At the Hebrew University and in other Israeli universities, work on the Holocaust was one theme among others, fairly well integrated into a broader program of studies and research. In the United States, a large number of institutions had developed the Holocaust as the central theme in a program of Jewish studies. As a result, I met a whole generation of younger American Jews who were well informed about the death of the Jewish people. Yet about Jewish life—its development, its history, its beliefs—they had learned next to nothing.

For too long I indulged in an overly simple explanation:

there was money available for Holocaust programs, and no director of Jewish studies in his right mind would relinquish it. In fact, the situation is more complex. The Holocaust was a major tragedy, and as such it appeals strongly to the sensibilities of American Jewry—apparently more than any other less evident (but not less important) issue in Jewish life. Nevertheless, despite this fixation, the Holocaust is the phenomenon in modern Jewish history that American Jews seem least prepared to deal with. It has a dimension that is basically alien to the American Jewish experience. American Jews are riding an upward trend in life, both as Americans and as Jews; they are optimistic and future-oriented. The Catastrophe, however, points in the opposite direction: downward, toward destruction and ruin.

Yet another aspect became for me a lesson in present-day Jewish Diaspora realities. However the various segments of modern Jewish society have coped with the influence of the Gentile environment, opinions of Gentile society have been an important reference point for Jewish views; these opinions have had a formative influence on Jewish behavior, especially in our time. To be blunt about it, modern Jews care what Gentiles think about them and how they react to their behavior. Gentile opinion has influenced, even shaped Jewish behavior. Observing how American Jewry dealt with the Holocaust issue, I began to see that here was a case where Jewish society was acting and reacting *without* the influence of Gentile society: few Gentiles dared to observe, certainly not in public, that Jewish attitudes about the Holocaust might be exaggerated, or tasteless, or worse.

I spoke about this with American colleagues. They shared my uneasiness, but felt powerless to alleviate it. My colleagues satisfied themselves with underground jokes. "No business like Shoah business," said (privately, of course) one Jewish professor, well-known for his black humor. But the jokes were self-defeating. In the end, the sad seed yielded a woeful harvest: the American Holocaust museums.

In the late 1980s, while I was in Germany, I read about proposals for Holocaust museums in Washington, New York and Los Angeles. Plans had been approved for the one in Washington, which would be built on the Mall, close to the Washington Memorial, in the very center of American national remembrance. A visitor entering the museum would receive a computerized card with the name of a "Doppelgänger," an accompanying shadow, someone of his or her age and gender who had perished in the

Holocaust. The visitor would see and hear pictures, movies, artifacts or sounds from the Holocaust: war scenes, cattle cars used for transporting prisoners, walls and fences, the crematoria, and the dead, the many dead. There would be a barracks where Jewish inmates had lived, a barracks brought from Poland and reassembled in the museum. The intention was to bring the visitor close to the "experience" of the Holocaust.

I found this appalling. Jewish tradition holds that the proper demeanor when facing death and sorrow is solemnity and restraint. American Jewish reactions to and about the Holocaust, as they were now intended to be expressed, were exactly the opposite: flamboyant, unrestrained, even aggressive. Considering the sites and the plans for these museums, it became evident to me that certain segments of American Jewry had reached the borders of intellectual or emotional disorientation in dealing with the Catastrophe.

The planned Holocaust museums moved me to action. I wrote a critical article analyzing their origins and pointing to their dangers. There was something deeply wrong, I wrote, in the way American Jewry was trying to depict the destruction of European Jewry. Those museums, I stated, were contrary to the Jewish tradition of mourning and remembering: they would be little more than an hour of contrived sorrow, of gimmickry and make-believe. Worse, I said, these plans indicated not sorrow for the destruction of European Jewry, but some darker and disruptive dimension in the soul of American Jewry itself.

"For the sake of our collective sanity as Jews," I wrote, "we should all stop for a moment, reflect about what is happening to us in that matter, and try to bring ourselves under control. The Holocaust museumania running wild in American Jewry is a latter-day expression, not about the Holocaust, but *of* the Holocaust."

The article was sent to two prestigious American Jewish magazines. Both journals, known for their supposed editorial independence, rejected it.

As deeply as I felt about what was happening among American Jews regarding the memory of the Holocaust, I had no doubt that a similar tendency existed in Israeli society, too, but with a disturbing difference: an Israeli expression of this attitude would be much more influential, since Israeli society was served by state structures and instruments to convey its opinions and feelings.

Some things were done well, I thought. Yad Vashem, the

Holocaust Memorial in Jerusalem, is dignified and, for the most part, decorous. The historical institute connected with Yad Vashem has fostered some excellent scholarly work. And the fact that the Day of the Holocaust is commemorated as an Israeli national day of sorrow and remembrance squares with Jewish tradition. However, like American Jewry, Israelis seem too self-absorbed in their own reactions and actions regarding the Holocaust. The attitude of many Israelis to the reunification of Germany, generally strident and negative, is one example of this self-absorption. We Jews have sometimes a weakness for doomsday preaching, a tendency stemming not so much from our prophetic tradition, as from our prophetic fashion. Some Israeli politicians stood up and thundered against German reunification as if they were reincarnations of Jeremiah. A few of my colleagues dismissed them as nitwits. I did not. One thing I have learned is that scholars should never underestimate politicians: they always have the last laugh.

But I was appalled by the sheer mindlessness of many Israeli reactions. There was no way, no way whatsoever, of knowing what the consequences of German reunification might be. One thing was clear: reunification was the result of another event, one that from any point of view—Jewish, human or social—was very positive and desirable: the collapse of communism in Eastern Europe.

A new Europe was taking shape before our eyes. It was with Europe that we Israelis, as a nation and as a society, were seeking contact, even integration—not that Europeans were so keen on the idea. We should adopt that point of view, emphasizing our present interests and future hopes, when considering what would be a problem for all Europeans: a new German colossus. The wisest thing one could do was wish the Germans good luck, and hope that the democratic structures erected in Western Germany since World War II would prove to be as solid as I hoped they were—a point on which many of my colleagues were less confident. To remain fixated on the past seems to me worse than futile. It is dangerous. As much as the fate of our parents and grandparents weighs on us, it is the future of our children and grandchildren that should determine our policies and actions.

ॐ

These practical observations and political conclusions, however, were built on personal considerations that I acknowledge are shaky and pessimistic. As I see it, more than the inner self-assurance of the Jewish people, which has been so central an anchor in hours of great need and sorrow, has been deeply disturbed. The Holocaust, in my view, left open crucial questions about the relationship between Jews and Gentiles, and I wonder if those questions are answerable. The historical evolution of European Jewry, a process of over one thousand years, led to Auschwitz—if the Germans were responsible, most other Europeans stood by, virtually impassive. No people can live in a vacuum, unrelated to the general human environment. I ask myself if the Holocaust has not called into question our existential condition in a way that stretches the limits of the endurable.

I pull myself together: tragedies in Jewish history, I tell myself, have happened before, and we have survived. In time, a new conception about Jewish life will develop—perhaps the process has already begun, in Israel? In time, in time. Yet there is no time, there never seems to be. Who can wait three or four centuries for the development of a new synthesis of Jewish life, such as occurred in medieval Spain, and later in Poland?

23

Germany, Fifty Years Later

Heidelberg was a city easy to live in. Closed in
between green mountains and the river Neckar, the city is small,
agreeable, soft. People in Heidelberg are known for their cordiality. The masses of students bicycling to and fro (the city's streets
make auto traffic an unmitigated mess) added an element of
crowded youthfulness. The Hochschule für Jüdische Studien,
where I was to teach during the academic year, is located in the
inner city, close to the university. I took a flat not far away and
bought a bicycle myself. The winter of 1989–90 was mild. It was
a daily pleasure to stroll or bike along the Neckar, the ruins of
the castle looming above.

My way back to Germany had been initiated about ten years
earlier, in relation to a curious reawakening of interest. In the
late 1970s, I had begun to work on the history of German Jewry.
While on a visit to London, I had the good fortune to meet
Arnold Paucker, the editor of the Leo Baeck Institute Year Book.
As Robert Weltsch's successor, Paucker was the right man at the
right moment: he transformed the Year Book into the focal point

of renewed academic interest in the history of Jews in Germany. A talk with him showed why: energetic and extremely positive, Paucker had a knack for helping one transform some still vague historical idea into a polished essay. Paucker also had a quality extremely rare among scholars: he was totally open-minded about criticism of his views.

In conjunction with my academic interest (but unrelated to it, I thought), I had had occasional meetings with Germans that were quite interesting. Many of them seemed exceedingly decent people. But beyond this, I felt a measure of empathy with them that should not have surprised me: obviously it had something to do with the remnant of my German past. Individual Germans, then, particularly Andreas Dorpalen, played an important role in my renewed inquisitiveness about matters German.

I met Dorpalen while teaching at Ohio State University in 1975–76. He was a senior figure in the Department of History, a well-known scholar in modern German history whose books on Treitschke and Bismarck were considered outstanding works in the field. Dorpalen left Germany in the Hitler years because he was an uncompromising liberal, and he settled in the United States. We had long conversations, and I wonder if he understood that for me he was like a door opening on a world that intrigued me very much.

Dorpalen was a most pleasant man: old-European manners, a kind sense of humor, patience without limits. There was only one issue that made me uncomfortable: there was something peculiar about his kind of liberalism. The liberalism I had experienced in Jewish circles (which was probably my own too), might not always be open-minded, but it certainly was flexible. Each of us might hold to beliefs he or she would be pretty dogmatic about, but most of us recognized that even the truths we regarded as sacred were, after all, relative. In addition, we had that saving human quality, a Jewish sense of humor. We were able to laugh at everything. Dorpalen, when the issue was liberalism, was quite inflexible. Then he became serious, rigid and, considering the man, rather humorless. Liberalism was for him a matter anchored in theory, in principle; no concessions were considered. I found his stance not only surprising, but also, if considered as a political or public attitude, rather unsettling.

❧

I had barely arrived in Germany, when two momentous events occurred: the collapse of communism in Eastern Europe and German reunification. I knew from the first moment that I was witnessing history, great history. In the two centuries since the French Revolution, efforts had frequently been made to reorganize or recreate human society according to one or another ideological blueprint. The year 1989 was a watershed for such attempts in Europe, with a general acceptance of a more sober and careful attitude toward tampering with social and political structures. As much as I welcomed the changes in Eastern Europe, I did so with mixed feelings. If the downfall of the communist regimes was to be cheered, what about the failure of the great dream of socialism? I could not fail to remember Bernard Shaw's words, that socialism expresses "the economist's hatred of waste and disorder, the aesthete's hatred of ugliness and dirt, the lawyer's hatred of injustice, the doctor's hatred of disease, the saint's hatred of the seven deadly sins." Was contemporary capitalism, even in its present, controlled, "socialized" form, an answer to humanity's problems? I doubted it. Even a restrained form of capitalism still depends for its survival on continual development, and where would that lead us? More than the failure of a political system, the crisis of socialism seemed to emphasize some characteristics of human nature that were less than admirable. The end of the communist regimes brought a sigh of relief to one's lips. But regarding the future, it promised nothing. And in the back of one's mind nagged some serious doubts.

In 1989 Europe was in flux. Where it was heading was unclear. Politicians, political scientists, sociologists, economists—all were running after the events. Predictions uttered today—and each day would bring new ones—were meaningless tomorrow. Indeed, it was a significant time in human history, and all of this was happening before one's very eyes. Most politicians showed themselves at their poorest, but here and there a figure emerged who for an hour or two became larger than life. I had a great deal of respect for Mikhail Gorbachev, the last president of the Soviet Union, leading his country into what he knew was a lost battle, but also an unavoidable proposition. Most of all, I came to admire the German chancellor, Helmut Kohl. Tall, corpulent, uneloquent, he seemed the incarnation of the middle-brow, beer-drinking German. "Der Dicke," the Fat One, cried the ferocious German weeklies, trying to laugh him away. I found their efforts silly: the man was revealing himself to be a masterful statesman. That Fat One knew how to ride the crest of a political wave like a true surfing champion. He managed that unbelievably complex task, the reunification of Germany, with an effortless aplomb which most of his political contemporaries did not fully comprehend. In the political confusion of the Eastern European debacle and the German upheaval, the man stood out like a rock. I had the impression then that Kohl would go down in German history as one of the greatest political figures of modern times.

Compared to all this, the quest that had brought me back to Germany was trivial indeed. But it was the right time to ask questions: queries about Germany were once again fair game.

The Hochschule für Jüdische Studien was an effort to recreate one of the establishments for Jewish higher learning that had existed in Germany until the 1930s. It was a worthwhile attempt, but the past, of course, cannot be recreated. The German and European Jewry which had given the older Judaic institution its sense and content was no more. Although its day-to-day schedule of studies implied regularity and order, the Hochschule was built upon several inner anomalies. It was a body established and maintained from above. The Central Council of the Jews in Germany bore formal responsibility for the Hochschule, but it was in no condition either to give academic orientation or deliver students in significant numbers. Heidelberg University provided the necessary academic backing and took a keen interest in that strangest of its connections, but it could hardly suggest what was a desirable academic direction for a program of Jewish studies. Most of the Hochschule faculty were German-speaking professors from Israel, many of them from the Hebrew University, who came for one or two semesters. In addition, there were some regular local teachers, but no truly permanent faculty had evolved after more than ten years.

Despite those limitations, the Hochschule was surprisingly alive. Strangely alive: the large majority of the approximately one hundred students were German Gentiles, many of them theology students. However, the Hochschule was one of the most Zionist-minded university institutions I have ever encountered in a Diaspora country. Many of the students had spent some time in Israel. All of them knew some Hebrew; some spoke it faultlessly. I have known Jews, especially American Jews, who, although they did not live in Israel, felt very much at home there: they had relatives and friends in Israel, visited it frequently, spoke Hebrew, mixed easily in the land and its society. To find that same phenomenon among Gentiles, and German ones at that, *was* surprising. As it was to see some blue-eyed German boy or girl sitting in the cramped library of the Hochschule over a large Talmudic treatise, pondering the intricacies of the ancient Aramaic and Hebrew texts. A new flower had grown on the troubled soil of the German-Jewish past. The Hochschule gave the impression of an institution poised for expansion. New developments in Germany and in Europe would probably cause further growth.

Once my rusty German began to flow more easily, my teaching presented no problems. The students were serious and interested. From time to time I was reminded that not everything was as simple as it seemed. In one of my classes there was a woman who obviously was not studying for a degree. Marianne Meyer-Krahmer had been the principal of a large Heidelberg school. She had been retired for some years, but as she was intellectually very keen, she took classes on issues that interested her. We spoke together, and I learned that Marianne was the daughter of Carl Goerdeler, who had been mayor of Leipzig in the 1930s and a very active opponent of Hitler and the Nazi regime. Goerdeler was one of the civilian leaders of the failed attempt to eliminate Hitler in June 1944. He was caught and executed in early 1945, several weeks before the collapse of the Nazi regime. Marianne was then in her mid-twenties. She and her family were thrown in prison, where they remained until the end of the war.

Hers was a perspective on Germany and German life I did not know: that of the too few Germans who stayed in Germany and resisted the Nazi regime. One would have thought that after the war ended life would be better for her and her family, but it had been otherwise. One had to remember that the Nazi regime was brought to an end only by total defeat and military occupation, not because of internal upheaval. Conditions in Germany after 1945 were hard for everybody, but especially for the Goerdelers. Were they not relatives of that traitor? Germans changed very slowly. Denazification was dilatory and had only a partial effect.

"How could you take it? Why did you not leave Germany?" I asked. We had become close enough to permit tough questions.

"Sometimes I wonder, too. It did not occur, we were too

busy trying to survive." Busy surviving: little did she know how well I understood her.

Marianne had trained as a high school teacher, and when the school year started in September 1945, she got a job in Stuttgart. "Clean" teachers were much sought after. She taught a class of girls seventeen or eighteen years old, many of whom had been leaders in the BDM, the Nazi youth organization for girls. There they had faced each other, students and teacher nearly the same age, children of two German worlds, both in ruins. Marianne read Goethe's *Werther* with the girls, a first step toward reeducating them with new human values.

In my second semester at the Hochschule I taught a course on modern German antisemitism with Eike Wolgast, a senior professor in the Department of History at Heidelberg University. We concentrated on the late nineteenth and early twentieth century. Wolgast was one of the foremost European specialists on Luther and his time, but he had also a deep knowledge of other periods of German history. He was a bachelor in his fifties, a devout Christian, retiring, ascetic, a man with a very high sense of duty, and extremely formal. We two, we got along famously. Beneath his severe exterior, Wolgast turned out to be the finest of men. His was a lucid intelligence, well served by that common sense which is such an essential quality in a historian. He was an ardent liberal whose ideas were tempered by a scepticism about human nature that matched my own. Last but not least, he had a fine sense of humor.

The class we taught together turned out to be quite an experience. There were about forty students, half from the university, half from the Hochschule, only a few of whom were Jewish. There we sat, session after session, analyzing German antisemitic texts according to the best rules of historical exegesis, well-behaved and objective.

"You know what is lacking here?" I said one day, "Apparently none of you has ever met a real, living antisemite. You do not know the species, with that peculiar look in his eyes, his peculiar stubbornness, his inner conviction that he knows the truth, even if he cannot always explain it logically." Wolgast winced, uneasy. He was right: my observation was outside the rules of historical discipline. The students looked at me, wide-eyed.

Another recollection from those first months in Heidelberg is attending a concert by the Jewish clarinetist, Giora Feidman. It was held in midwinter, and the large city concert hall was completely full. Feidman played Eastern European Jewish tunes and gradually the audience warmed up. Soon they were humming along with the clarinet. And there I sat, dumbfounded, listening to a German public singing *hasidic* melodies, asking myself: now, what is *that* supposed to mean?

ᐁ

Much later, when I was back in Israel, I recognized how my life in Heidelberg, especially at the beginning, moved back and forth between strangely related levels of interest and awareness. One level was my day-to-day life, apparently regular, apparently comfortable. Another level, almost part of the first, was my work at the Hochschule, also quite pleasant. In fact, everything was much more complex than it appeared to be. I had been, literally, sniffing around, trying to catch impressions, faces, behaviors, with sharpened intellectual and emotional faculties. Looking back from that later perspective, it became evident that during that first period I was under severe stress. This was hardly a frame of mind apt to serve my quest—to understand (whatever that meant) Germans and Germany. I was on too personal a track. Germans, and especially Germans in Heidelberg, lived according to a completely different rhythm. I had no way of connecting my restless heart and strained mind to their rather placid and well-ordered way of life. Only after several months had passed—and then with the help of a German friend, vital and sensitive, who grasped what was happening to me and knew how to extend a helping hand—did I regain some inner balance.

I have learned that a useful way to orient myself in a new country is to seek contact with the local Jews. Usually, our common Jewishness acts like a bridge to an environment I am not yet familiar with. This tactic functioned extremely well when I lived in America. In Germany, it did not work. When I had been in Heidelberg for over six months, travelling to different places and coming in contact with many people, I realized that I was having more successful, sustained contact with Gentiles than with Jews. This was strange: in the United States the opposite had been true.

At first I attributed this to some subjective inhibition on my part, although I did not share the negative opinion held by many Israelis about the reestablishment of Jewish life and the organization of Jewish communities in Germany. I believe that wherever Jews choose to live, they should organize themselves in communities; furthermore, we should help them in their Jewish endeavors. Indeed, I frequently met Jews who were active in German Jewish communal life. They were dedicated to their task and we had some thoughtful talks. Why then did I react as I did? Apparently at least in part because of the negative impressions I received from my Jewish interlocutors in Germany. There was an overall sense of disorientation and hopelessness, even among those who were professionally engaged in Jewish communal work. The majority of those Jews were not German-born, and thus they did not have a sense of stability in the country. They would frequently tell me, without having been asked, that they were going to move to Israel sooner or later. The level of "outmarriages" among Jews in Germany was very high, the number of children very low, and the median age of most of the German Jewish communities was catastrophic. German Jewry—where was it going? The implicit answer seemed to be, nowhere. This does not mean that Jews in Germany, or at least some of them, were not organizing their communities and maintaining Jewish traditions. Despite the negative atmosphere, it would not surprise me to find German Jewry, one or two decades later, expanded and even more active. Whether it would be more optimistic was another question.

Obviously, everyone was concerned with the definition or sense of Jewish life in Germany. This was a theme I never brought up in conversations with German Jews; it would only have caused embarrassment. But the question was there and permeated every step and thought relating to Jewish activities in Germany. The Jews who coped with it best were those who simply did not try to answer it, but lived their day-to-day lives and participated in Jewish activities according to the old traditions of Jewish existence.

But those who did engage the issue were often remarkable! Participating in a symposium on Jewish life in Bavaria, I met a German Jewish professor who was considered by many an expert on the issue of the German-Israeli-Jewish situation. Although German-educated, he had been born in Israel, and had even returned there to do military service. He brought up that fact on every possible occasion, something no real Israeli would do: it certainly was the most useful military service I had ever heard about. Because of his ties with all three angles of the German-Jewish issue, he considered himself well prepared to propose what he thought was a less biased solution to the problem. In his opinion, there were already normal relations between the Germans and the Jews. But politicians and ideologists on both sides, for whatever dark reasons and interests, refused to recognize the facts of life.

At the particular symposium where we met, the theme of his lecture was the history of the Jews in Regensburg, an important Bavarian Jewish community in the Middle Ages. His talk went peacefully enough, until the point where, through some feat of intellectual gymnastics that I did not exactly grasp (after all, the medieval Jewish community in Regensburg ceased to exist in 1519), the professor introduced some comments about the plight of Palestinians in contemporary Israel. He soon followed these with remarks about the nonexistence of any guilt factor in present-day relations between Germans and Jews. He was provocative and irritating. People rose and left the session in protest. I asked him if he was treating the issue of guilt from the German or the Jewish perspective. Even God could not do it from both. The poor moderator, a German historian taken completely unaware by what had happened, stared with open mouth at the mess that had fallen into his lap, unable to decide where and how to stop the confrontation.

After the close of the session I had an opportunity for a personal talk with the professor. He wasn't a bad person, only an extreme example of the confusion that frequently befuddled discussions of the German-Jewish question. His attitude betrayed the kind of superficiality one finds sometimes among people who deal with contemporary issues and believe that matters are just as they appear before our eyes. Whatever may be behind them, the deeper historical, spiritual, or ideological roots of present-day phenomena—well, this was a question of interpretation, wasn't it?

Indeed, it was, but in a much more complex way than he was able to avow. Beneath the comfortable day-to-day life in Germany there was another level of awareness, which I found expressed in the more serious German press or in contacts with German acquaintances who were Gentiles: an undercurrent of unrest about the German past in general and about the German-Jewish question. Later, those preoccupations were compounded by worries about what might happen in a reunified Germany.

This level of life in Germany interested me deeply. However, my first reaction was to be careful, to keep my distance. Many of my Israeli or Jewish colleagues behaved the same way. Why? Because the issue was too complicated, or too painful; or because one understood early enough that whatever active role a Jew could fulfill in the German-Jewish situation, it was limited to the Jewish side. Regarding the Germans, all one could do was observe, ponder, conclude, and sometimes, when asked, inform.

One might think that such a conclusion was pretty obvious. It was not. It was surprising how many Jews, in Israel or in the Diaspora, were unable to accept the fact that the impact of our attitudes and reactions regarding life in the post-Holocaust era was confined to ourselves. Many of us were so conditioned by our involvement in the Jewish-German problem that it was an effort to grasp our limitations. The media, too, both local and international, heightened that confusion by emphasizing Jewish reactions to German issues. It was nothing but a mirage. Half a century after the Holocaust, Jews and Germans, however interested and sensitive about what had happened in Nazi times, lived in completely separate political and human spheres. It was unreasonable to expect present-day Germans to understand the deeper complexities of current Israeli political, social or religious life. We ourselves hardly understood them! And how well could a Jew or an Israeli grasp the currents and sub-currents of German reality?

As members of different societies, Jews and Germans could relate to each other only within obvious limits. This did not mean that the past was forgotten. Far from it: I had yet to discover how significant it still was. But it did mean that confrontation with the past happened only within each group, and according to ways and rules that were peculiar to each side.

For me, it became clear that any other understanding of the Jewish-German issue would likely lead to disappointment and intellectual confusion. Later I grasped something else: strange as it seemed, that seemingly modest point of departure opened the possibility—if one deemed it worthwhile—of a new and sometimes very significant contact between Jews and Germans.

24

Through Jewish Eyes

At the beginning, then, I was no more than an observer in Germany, although an uncommonly interested one.

Most contemporary Germans, I found, were much less concerned about the German-Jewish past than their Jewish counterparts were. Not that all Germans were oblivious to Nazi crimes against the Jews, against all the others. Life, however, had gone on. Germany was in upheaval, Europe in transformation. The dark side of the German past, worrisome, unexplained, inexplicable, was only one of many components in the larger mosaic of German self-understanding.

Among contemporary Germans there were several groups whose awareness about the German past and the German-Jewish past (obviously, the two were not necessarily related) was more highly developed. My attention was first drawn to a group which Jews found highly irritating: German intellectuals, mostly historians, who were engaged in reinterpreting the Holocaust. Their position had been highlighted in the so-called "historians' debate" that had flared up in the mid-1980s.

Their effort had not been initiated by any original reflections about the destruction of European Jewry in the 1940s. Politicians, especially from the conservative camp, had been commenting on the lack of national pride that characterized most Germans in the 1980s. The root of the problem, responded the listening historians, was that Germans were shy about coping with recent German history. National awareness did not tolerate spots historically empty, the most notorious of which, for Germans, was the period of the Third Reich. This period, too, ought to be incorporated into an overall view of the German past.

Basically, this intention was legitimate. It is the task of the historian to help elaborate his people's past. We Jewish historians were also engaged in a similar effort to comprehend our recent history. However, the German historians' pursuit demanded great maturity and even greater moral courage. The complexity of the issue became evident when I read Karl Jaspers' *The Question of Guilt,* a monograph based on lectures he gave in Heidelberg in 1945–46, shortly after returning from exile.

Jaspers' was a clear-headed treatment of the theme of German guilt, and it made sobering reading. His moral categories were lucid, uncorrupted and, considering their time, pitiless. It was difficult to find a harsher view of German conduct during the Hitler years, expressed by a German. Still, the way Jaspers dealt with it, German guilt was transformed into a theoretical category. No specific word was said, no specific feeling uttered, about the sufferings of Jews, Poles, Gypsies, Russians, or any of the other peoples subjugated by the Germans during the war. No mention of the burned-out villages, the butchery carried out by the *Einsatzgruppen,* the systematic scientific extermination. This absence was all the more baffling because the Jaspers who glimmered throughout the essay appeared to be a sensitive man. Nevertheless, his intellectual aim seemed to be the systematization of German guilt: dividing it into categories; distinguishing between collective and individual guilt; between violence, right and mercy; assessing the right relation between causes and consequences, the ways that would lead to a moral cleansing of the Germans. In the end, it was very intelligent—and almost inhuman. Whatever feelings managed to trickle through were reserved for the Germans. For the Jews, for all the other victims, there was almost nothing.

Whatever reservations I had about Jaspers' position, his moral integrity was beyond doubt. With regard to the participants in the "historians' dispute," the situation was not so clear. They espoused theoretical concepts that were in themselves statements, such as the "normalization" of the German past. But normalization quickly stumbled on a difficult obstacle, the Holocaust. The extermination of European Jewry was so singular an event that it simply could not be incorporated into an ordered, "normal" view of German history. It did not take long for some German historians to suggest that the Holocaust was not, after all, so bizarre or unique an occurence. Had not Stalin killed tens of millions in the Siberian Gulag camps? Had not one-third of the Cambodian population been exterminated by the Khmer Rouge? The destruction of European Jewry, it was now suggested, was but one example—only one among others, and not even the first one—of how modern ideology and technology could foster levels of human destruction unheard of before.

There is no language like German for smoke-screening an issue. But once some of those statements were translated into English, the intention behind the elaborate German sentences was plain. Here once again were the old arrogance of certain Germans, the capacity for masking nationalistic aspirations behind high-sounding, obtuse formulations. "Normalization," "to come to terms with the past," and similar concepts mostly meant the same thing: to get rid of the moral burdens of the Nazi period, of which the most burdensome was the long shadow of Auschwitz.

Another example of a (in my view) problematic approach to the Nazi period is the treatment by German historians (and by some non-German ones, too) of that most strange figure, Adolf Hitler—whom I had seen and heard, I was almost sure now, when I was a child. During the year I spent in Heidelberg I read quite a number of works about him, and they filled me with an increasing sense of perplexity regarding the man, his ideas, his actions—and his biographers. Almost all German scholars tended to distance themselves from Hitler. Understandably, the more critical the opinion about Hitler, the greater the distancing. Frequently such opinions reflected genuine moral revulsion against the man and his doings, but in some cases I was left in doubt. It was easy, too easy, to represent Germans as the victims of a demonic creature who had inflicted unaccountable harm on Germany as well as on others. Gradually I leaned toward quite a different view. The more I pondered Hitler, the more his personal contours became blurred, mixed up with my comprehension of the broader historical context, namely, Germany in the 1930s.

I remembered a conversation I once had in the mid-1980s with Hans Mommsen, a leading German historian of the Nazi period. Mommsen had described how disorganized, even chaotic, Hitler's style of life was: a late-riser (especially after he had harangued an audience of adepts and visitors until the small hours of the morning); uninterested in organizational details; very busy with the internal quarrels among that weird cluster of his close Nazi associates; frequently moody, frequently lazy. In fact, Hitler was a most unlikely figure to reach the top of German political life: an Austrian (most of my German acquaintances had less than an enthusiastic opinion about Austrians), declassé, with no formal education. The last man, one would suppose, to be accepted into the tradition-minded, well established and quite formal structures of German society and the German state.

All this made his political accomplishment in 1933 even more astonishing. In less than six months, Hitler and the bunch of political amateurs around him—many of them bizarre people, most inexperienced in public administration—had, one was told, "crushed" all the political frameworks of Germany, "taken over" the public machinery, "cowed" the universities, the army, the police, the juridical system. All this smoothly and faultlessly—so faultlessly smoothly that one began to wonder.

My doubts were raised even more by the trouble I had with accepted descriptions of the "desperate" state of Germany in 1932–33; this critical situation had made it possible, so one was told, for Hitler to reach for the chancellorship. Indeed, how desperate could the situation have been, how sick the German nation, if within the space of a few years the Germans were able to put together one of the most formidable military machines in history, sustained by a nation that was closely united and highly supportive of its Nazi leadership?

Gradually I developed the impression that the person Hitler, rather than a political creator, had been an instrument. An instrument of a certain dimension in the German national identity, which had affirmed itself from 1933 onward, the result of the merging of certain ideological trends, economic circumstances, social conditions and political problems. This was a dark and worrisome dimension, expressing itself as a destructive (and, in the end, self-destructive) rampage by the German people—a *sitra ahra*, as the kabbalist concept goes. It seemed one possible explanation for the complete identity of a large majority of Germans with such an improbable man. Most Germans had gone along too gladly with Hitler—or was it Hitler who had gone with them?— from step to step, outrage to outrage, evil to evil, all the while convinced and enthusiastic. They had taken part in the expulsion or the slaughter of the Jews, the German socialists, the communists, the liberals. They participated in aggression against other peoples in Europe, brutal submission, abuse. Not until the Stalingrad debacle, in the winter of 1942–43, did the very close identification between most Germans and Hitler begin to show its first fissures. By then it was too late. The Germans were in the hands of a "golem," a creature, a monster of their own creation in their own image.

In other words, it seemed to me that Hitler could not be separated from the German people. The key to understanding the man had to be sought, in my view, among Germans themselves. Obviously, this is a highly subjective interpretation, yet not unrelated to my professional experience as a historian. If I found myself employing concepts that were not precise enough, it was because the situation I was trying to grasp became increasingly complex, the deeper I got into it through certain avenues.

With such thoughts in mind, I considered the public discussion that had erupted in Germany in the 1980s about the Nazi period. I wondered if some old demons were not too deeply imbedded in some parts of German society to simply disappear in one or two generations. Sometimes one could still glimpse their ugly tails. One demon, an apparently innocuous one, which I had become particularly sensitive to, was the tendency toward abstraction, that love for ideas, for systematizing issues at the expense of meaning in life, where blood and suffering were at least as important as the right formulation of the matter. I sniffed this demon the first time during my talks with Dorpalen, the too-perfect liberal. I sensed it again while reading Jaspers, the too-perfect moralist. In the "historians' dispute" that tendency reappeared full-blown, this time neither perfect, nor liberal, nor moral.

It is important to note that during the "historians' debate" several eminent German historians reacted with great indignation, fueled by much worry, against this new, revisionist trend. They all stressed, each in his own way, the terrible significance of National-Socialist antisemitism and the uniqueness of the German crime against the Jewish people. I respected their honesty, but still I did not feel comfortable. The idea that we Jews had been the victims of a "unique" crime is a dubious honor I have never been ready to insist upon. Suffering is suffering and murder is murder, be it against Jews, Russians, Cambodians or any other human group. To my understanding, the truly monstrous feature of the Holocaust was the distinctive, nay, the absolute moral perversion it imbued: the idea that for the greater happiness of humanity in general and of the German people in particular it was imperative to exterminate the Jews, each one of them and all together. That a majority of the German people—men, women, priests, bureaucrats, soldiers and civilians—listened to such an "ideal," considered it and, in thousands of cases, participated actively in its realization.

By 1990, when I was in Germany, the "historians' dispute" seemed to have calmed down. Historians and everybody else were busy with what was happening in Eastern Europe in general and in Eastern Germany in particular. However, I had an acute feeling that the dispute in the mid-eighties was only one round in a discussion that would flare up again, especially after the unification of Germany was accomplished. The fight for the German soul is, in my opinion, a chapter not yet complete. But it is an issue we Jews can only observe with astonishment, and Germany's neighbors with preoccupation. In the end, it is a matter the Germans themselves will have to confront.

∾

All this, however, represented only one part of my impressions of modern Germany. There was another side to the coin. The spiritual and political evolution of Western Germany has been such that the German-Jewish past can no longer be swept under the carpet, as had happened in Eastern Germany during the decades of the communist regime. Something had changed in Germany, although precisely what was not easy to explain, especially since many Germans denied that new ideals had arisen in German life or public opinion. Germany, one was told in 1990, had become a non-ideological country. What mattered now was the good life, vacations in Spain, a new Volkswagen— or perhaps, finally, a new Mercedes. The only national fervor that fueled German reunification, I was told, was economic interest. "Deutschmark nationalism," it was derogatorily called. Nobody bothered any longer about ideological or national values, it was said—by some with indifference, by others with regret.

I wondered. First because there are segments in German

society, on both the right and the left of the political spectrum, that are intensely interested in ideology. People alluded to the threat of the neo-Nazis, the so-called Republicans. One of my ideological disillusions in Germany, in the late 1980s, was with respect to some members of the "Greens." At that time, they were morally sensitive, yet many among them were politically immature, dogmatic, and seemed to have a veritable instinct for misguided decisions (they were to improve later). My general impression was that there were types of ideological Germans who might become, in certain circumstances, either politically unreliable or even dangerous.

Second, it seemed to me that the development of the non-ideological German was not the result of ideological apathy, but rather the contrary: such development represented an ideological creation in itself, and a most important one. This evolution happened within the broad center of German society and included people who belonged to diverse political parties. It was closer to an attitude than a formulated position, based more on instinct and experience than on clear political constructs. However, its adherents had learned a very basic lesson: not to trust their ideological selves and to be wary of ideologies in general, especially in Germany. The new German mind is, in my opinion, the result of forty years of quiet self-education and maturation. It is a notable development, everything considered: neither the schools nor political events seem to have played a decisive role in that evolution. These non-ideological people do not recognize what they have attained, but in my view they are the bearers of a new German consciousness, a balanced dimension in German public behavior.

How strong is this new German non-ideological ideology? The next few years will tell, after the consequences of German reunification have filtered through and become part of German self-awareness. It is my hope that the social and political checks and balances that have developed in Western Germany will prove strong enough to preserve that precious middle ground in German public life—and be resilient enough to cope with the old German demons.

In that same central part of German society I found a group that, in addition to having attained a non-ideological consciousness, was particularly sensitive to the German-Jewish issue. This group was not without influence, but it seemed small. Later I found that it was much larger than I had thought. It represented an entire segment of German public opinion, but among those Germans there were diverse levels of awareness or activity. It encompassed several age groups. Many of its members were people of my generation, but many were youngsters, like the students at the Hochschule. Many were believing Christians, Catholics or Protestants. What I found significant was that these Germans had not simply remained aware of the burden of the German-Jewish question, they had confronted it: they had looked at their not-too-distant history and recoiled in horror. Their outrage at the Jewish tragedy in Germany was not a one-time matter, but a continuing process. In recent years the impact of the German past on that group seems to be increasing.

My contact with these Germans was one of the main stimulants that led me to ponder again the relationship between Jews and Germans. From that point on, I was drawn into a sequence of questions and answers on the Jewish-German issue that were far from simple. The intensity of the process was surprising: I felt like one of those people who paddle down a river in a small boat, in increasingly turbulent waters. There was no stepping-off place. One had to finish the rocky course. From being an observer I had become, in a limited or not so limited sense, a participant.

25

Jews and Germans

Neither the thoughts I had about Germans and the Jewish-German question in 1989–90, nor the conclusions I arrived at, came to me in the order in which I have described them here. They were originally as diffuse as my experiences that year. There was the original, professional quest that brought me to Germany, a historical understanding of the Jewish-German relationship. There was the matter of my own German past: there was a German dimension to my childhood that I was trying to "localize" better. There were also personal relations with Germans, which influenced my feelings and thoughts. There were issues I had dealt with in the past and that had now reemerged. There were ideas I resisted, when they first dawned on me. Any order in my thoughts and perceptions came later, gradually.

Frequently, reflection would begin after a conversation with certain Germans had left an intriguing impression. I would have a lingering sense that there was something more to be said. This generally happened in Germany itself. Meetings elsewhere, especially in Israel, were much easier; usually cordial, but careful. In Germany, conversations hardly ever started with the more serious issues. One observed limits, particularly at the beginning of friendships, out of embarrassment, or because it was so difficult to formulate questions.

This experience led me to the first stage of my probe into the Jewish-German issue. It seemed obvious to me that some Germans were trying to reach us. They had a problem; they were attempting to understand their past and themselves, their "German-ness." Should we engage them? Or should we, the Jews, follow until the end of our days the biblical injunction: "Remember, remember what Amalek did to you!" Was it not a much more honorable solution to leave the lines between Germans and Jews drawn as they were: for some inexplicable, for others a continuing accusation? Did not present political and social forms offer an acceptable framework, at least tolerable for both sides, for the Jewish-German relationship?

Obviously, I am not the first Jew or Israeli to face questions of this kind. Jewish literature dealing with the post-Holocaust situation fills a whole library. However, it provided very little orientation for my particular quest. My first engagement in the contemporary German-Jewish issue was rather negative, although passive. It occurred during the German "historians' debate" of the 1980s. My colleagues' reactions were characterized by a fine-honed perception of each trivial intellectual ruse some of the German historians were employing to shrug off that burden, the Holocaust. Usually my colleagues were right on target. However, this time it was not discussion we were engaged in, but confrontation.

Confrontation is easier than encounter. In an encounter one deals with men and women, living ones, not only with situations. And what is to be gained by scraping away at the wounds of the Jewish-German past? If one came into closer contact with Germans, might one not end up getting trapped again in the unacceptable situation Gershom Sholem warned against, when he thundered about the illusions of the Jewish-German encounter in modern times? "I deny that there has ever been such a German-Jewish dialogue in any genuine sense whatsoever, i.e., *as a historical phenomenon*," he wrote in 1962:

It takes two to have a dialogue, who listen to each other, who are prepared to perceive the other as what he is and represents, and to respond to him. Nothing can be more misleading than to apply such a concept to the discussions between Germans and

Jews during the last 200 years. This dialogue died at its very start and never took place. . . . When they [the Jews] thought they were speaking to the Germans, they were speaking to themselves. . . . The allegedly indestructible community of the German essence with the Jewish essence consisted, so long as these two essences really lived with each other, only of a chorus of Jewish voices and was, on the level of historical reality, never anything else than a fiction. . . .

Although Sholem's reasoning is similar to the approach of most Zionist thinkers who have analysed the modern Jewish-European (or Jewish-German) historical encounter, I have never been able to accept it. It presumes a kind of intellectual barter between the sides, Jews and Germans, that simply does not exist in real life. The fierceness of the debate among Jewish historians over the Jewish-German issue has obscured the fundamental fact that the encounter did not happen because of one ideological-cultural intention or another, but because it was historically unavoidable. It was a result of modernization and reflected the broader internal dynamics of European society. It did not occur because of the Jews, or because of the Germans, or in order to serve one side or the other. Whether a dialogue ever developed between Jews and Germans—this was another question, certainly a most interesting one, but hardly determinant of the historical process itself.

My point of intellectual departure was a different one. Long before traveling to Germany, I understood that comprehension of the sources and motivations behind the Catastrophe is vitally needed in present-day Jewish life. It is an indispensable dimension in our effort to reconstruct terms of spiritual and social reference for ourselves amid the conditions of the contemporary world. If the encounter with Germans helped in the pursuit of that quest, the encounter seemed justified: it happened for our own sake, as Jews. Evidently, some similar logic worked also from the German side, regarding a dialogue with Jews. Primarily, then, it is neither curiosity, nor the longing for revenge, nor guilt, nor the more rarified reasons of historical research *per se*— each side with its own motivations—that were the impelling reasons for mutual contact. It was the possibility, through a closer knowledge of the other side, of understanding better what had happened to ourselves.

There was, however, one more reason for me to continue

my quest: once in Germany, I could no longer avoid inquiring. When I decided to go to Germany it had been clear to me that if I behaved like an anthropologist examining a strange species, *homo germanicus*, I would never understand anything. I had to live in Germany fully and without preconditions, and accept Germans as they were. More, I needed to depend on whatever German dimension remained from my past if I hoped to expand my level of communication with Germans. What I did not know was how unavoidably I would be drawn to the great, the mutually painful issues.

∾

If contact with Germans, contact with which ones? This raised an issue which, in the final analysis, has become for me the crucial one: should I relate to individual Germans or to Germans as a group? Can two groups of people talk? How could I combine, or at least synchronize, those two levels, the individual and the collective? Issues in the German-Jewish problem that, if not easy, seem at least definable and clear from an individual perspective, appear nebulous and fickle when considered from a collective angle. If the collective level of communication remained hazy, would not personal contact lose any possibility of deeper significance?

Indirectly, some elements of that question had been on my mind for a long time, ever since I had read Hannah Arendt's controversial monograph, *Eichmann in Jerusalem*. The general indignation caused in its time by her essay had left me rather untouched. I thought that Arendt had put her finger on a very real and disturbing question: the issue of personal and collective guilt. An effort was required to accept her remarkable insights, because the Arendt-persona that one glimpses through the book is not very likable. She seems driven by obscure passions in which one can sense a strong measure of Jewish self-hatred. Now Jewish self-hatred is a recurring phenomenon in modern Jewish history; sometimes it is a problematic by-product of the process of the integration of Jews into Gentile society. As such, it should be recognized and understood, and one should be as clear-headed and direct about it as possible. Hannah Arendt was neither.

However, the idea of the "banality of evil," to use Arendt's expression, has much truth in it. Eichmann, that thin little man I observed carefully, sitting there in the glass box, in the courtroom in Jerusalem—he was supposed to be the incarnation of absolute evil? Evil was much too elevated a category for what I saw and heard. Eichmann impressed me as little more than a typical German bureaucrat, efficient and dedicated, one like thousands of others of his time, trying to do a good "job." I doubted how much he understood of the complexities of the German-Jewish situation, or how much he cared. The three judges, led by the impressive Moshe Landau, were indeed caught in an impossible dilemma: to personalize a crime where the personal dimension, although existent and damnable, was far from the real issue. The judges could only apply their categories of judicial thought, the result of centuries of Jewish and Western experience, to a situation that could hardly be encompassed by those categories. In fact, Eichmann became a symbol, and as such he was condemned and hanged. As far as symbols have significance, his death was, in my opinion, significant—and may he burn in hell, I thought. But guidelines for comprehending the German-Jewish relationship, in the past or in the present, did not and could not rise out of Eichmann's trial and subsequent death. All the larger issues of the German-Jewish problem, those touching on reasons for the Catastrophe, or those moral and metaphysical matters such as guilt and redemption, punishment and reconciliation, remained as unsolved as ever.

Who, however, could have claimed that such questions would be solved by the Eichmann trial? Besides punishing Eichmann himself, what else was intended beyond creating a symbolic situation? Neither in the Eichmann trial, nor in the Nuremberg trials, nor in any other trials against Nazis was more attained than the punishment of individual culprits. The broader crime would be condemned only by implication.

Those were my conclusions years ago when I first speculated about Hannah Arendt's monograph and the Eichmann trial. Reconsidering these events then, I realized that the judicial approach did not offer, as such, real guidance for the Jewish-German situation. Judicial decisions do not deal in metaphysical right or wrong. Legal decisions are practical: they aim to establish the personal guilt of a given individual and decide his punishment, which must be measurable in human, individual terms. They may imply or even explicate the responsibility of the group within whose structure and in whose name an individual acted. However, at that point the juridical instrument loses its cutting edge, since it is doubtful how "legal" collective punishment is. And if we doubt the legality of the punishment, what sense is there, from the point of view of my quest, in the juridical solution?

These conclusions do not upset me, because they square with my experience in historical work. It is both the strength and the weakness of law—a historian is confronted by this time and again—that it can only express the morals and the values of organized society and serve them—whatever they may be. High-flown rhetoric about the law apart, there has never been a ruler who had any trouble finding judges to apply his laws, no matter how unjust and wicked these laws might be. There is no need to search very far for examples. Take the case of Eastern European countries, where the juridical apparatus served first one political and ideological system, and then shortly afterwards, with the collapse of communism in the early 1990s, adapted itself to different and in some cases even opposite political regimes—and all this smoothly and without visible qualms. I do not, of course, reject the juridical approach in general. I think that one should accept it for what it is worth, without nursing illusions about it. But for my quest then—Jews and Germans, fifty years later—it offered little help or orientation.

If not the legal approach, what else? Looking here and there I found that the theologian Paul Tillich had expressed some interesting ideas about the issue of individual and collective guilt. Tillich was aware of the contradictions of the question. Situations of collective guilt, he stated (obviously thinking about the Germans), sometimes encompassed those who were innocent, even those who had resisted the crimes committed, and suffered because of their resistance. Tillich reached a not uncommon and quite logical conclusion: that collective guilt is an impossible concept, and that a social group as such cannot be either estranged or forgiven. His solution for the moral problem thus created was to reach for a new concept: destiny. Destiny, as Tillich explained it, means the all-encompassing human condition, and it rules all, the group as well as the individual. The individual participates, not in the guilt of his nation or of his group, but in its destiny.

Tillich's argument seemed to me unconvincing. Destiny is a notion of haunting human significance, but in most fields of rational thought and knowledge it has little meaning. Destiny is especially devoid of significance in any frame of thought related to a scale of values. Therefore it struck me as particularly out of place in a theological approach. I had the impression that the theologian, having found no guidance in his ideological arsenal, looked for help somewhere else. I remained left with the unsolved question of collective guilt.

At least the intellectual limitations of my quest seemed to have become clearer. It is evident that whatever sense of values underlie our existence, it draws its purport and effectiveness from the individual dimension, from moral principles built on concepts about the relationship between man and, let us say, God, and resonating from there between man and man. Guilt, expiation, repentance, forgiveness—they are all individual categories. Their meaning on a social or collective plane is only a reflection of their significance on the individual plane. As reflections they are rather static and passive.

If static and passive, how meaningful can they be? What demands can be put upon them? Within the framework of my particular quest about Jews and Germans, this question demanded clear answers. As I came to see it, the nebulous links connecting the individual and social dimensions of our lives cannot justify any weakening of the exigencies requiring moral behavior on some plane or other. If we do not have better moral criteria, we must employ the existing ones, drawn from the individual sphere, in spite of their imperfections. The alternative is chaos. Consequently, injustice is injustice and murder is murder, in the individual as well as in the collective sphere. To recognize the complexity of the human condition is one thing. To relativize our norms of behavior because of it is another. Moral principles on the collective level are static and passive, but devoid of meaning they are not.

Abstractly formulated, that trend of thought seemed logical. Applied to life—in our case, to the Jewish-German question—it was a tough proposition: in principle there were no moral or intellectual tools to open a path away from condemning Germans as a group. The German people as such bore responsibility for the Holocaust and for participating in it. Most Germans had identified with the Nazi regime to a degree that was now usually downplayed. In historical perspective, however, there could be little doubt about this identification. The German people accepted Hitler in 1933, participated in the upbuilding of the Nazi regime, acquiesced all too indifferently (if not gladly) to the long list of infamous acts, took part in the war. They also participated in the

Extermination, even if most of them never touched one hair of a Jew. Even those Germans who were personally innocent—indeed, those who had themselves been victims of the Nazi regime—still shared moral responsibility for the crime.

As logical, nay, as unavoidable as these conclusions seemed, they had about them something inhuman. True, they enabled one to take a stand on the issue of collective guilt. But collective guilt, I had come to understand, was not a category in itself; it was only a reflection of the moral idea of individual guilt. Consequently, it afforded no expiation. There is no possible interaction between personal and collective forgiveness: no individual can forgive a whole group, or do so in the name of a whole group. Collective guilt, then, was permanent and irreparable. If so, did this not empty it of its meaning? Worse, there was a sense of vindictiveness about collective guilt that in the long run did the victims at least as much harm as it did the perpetrators, since it kept the victims sealed off forever in their own misery.

In the final analysis, it added up to an intellectual and emotional situation that, although logical, was disturbing. Questions and answers that lead to an intellectual cul-de-sac always leave me uneasy. Could that Gordian knot be severed? I hesitated. At that point, I recalled a situation and a remark from my distant past: in 1955, in the western Negev, in the ditches near kibbutz Urim where that group of Jewish Kurds and I had been talking, while taking cover from Egyptian fire. "But we are Jews!" their leader had declared, commenting on a problem they were having in their village. Indeed, we were. Between strict logic and high morals, it was toward *"mentshlekhkeyt"* (humanity, in Yiddish), that my Jewish self impelled me.

The nub of the matter, I concluded, was this: were there Germans, individual Germans, who assumed blame for what had happened to the Jews in Nazi times? Moral responsibility is something that must be taken, not imposed. The moment one tries to force guilt and responsibility on someone else it is emptied of significance: we are back to a juridical situation, and farther away from a moral one.

There were such Germans. Indeed, they had been part of the first impulse leading me toward my search. There can be links of personal contact and dialogue within the level of collective consciousness, although they may be difficult to pinpoint. Dialogue between individuals is like a laboratory where new thoughts are elaborated, which in some way will eventually have a formative influence on broader public opinion. The fact that we do not understand well enough the dynamics of those influences did not justify doubts about their existence and importance.

I decided to engage in dialogue. This was my own private resolution; I did not impose it on anyone else. Whoever disagreed was free to adopt the contrary position—not to enter into contact with Germans—and this decision would be as legitimate as mine. The small wedge keeping open a means of communication and mutual influence between these almost unsolvable propositions was personal dialogue between Jew and German. Dialogue meant not only, or even necessarily, the exchange of ideas on the elevated level of intellectual discussion, like considering matters relating to the history of the Jews in Germany and the history of the Catastrophe. Dialogue should also include personal contact that might allow a Jew to gain insight into what had happened from the perspective of one's German interlocutor. It meant sharing ideas, experiences and feelings. Behind this effort was an intriguing question: could it be that dealing with our past, instead of separating us, might construct a fragile bridge between us?

The process of dialogue, I found, was difficult and frequently self-defeating. Conversations would often go along the following lines:

"Herr Wolgast, I look around me, and I cannot understand: how could it have happened?"

"Of course, Herr Friesel. You look around you, and all you see is a perfectly normal bunch of people walking in the streets."

"But these 'perfectly normal people,' or others, like you and me, they could have walked these same streets fifty years ago, exactly the same. And acted or suffered as it indeed happened!"

He shrugged, perplexed. He could not understand it either.

If there was an answer, it eluded us. It seemed, however, that the essence of the quest was raising the question, and in the human exchange. The dialogue itself mattered. True dialogue would begin only after careful probing and much hesitation. The question, not the answer, became the bridge between the two sides.

But dialogue for its own sake, dialogue without a clear purpose, without aiming for a convincing answer? Was there not a disproportion between the tension generated by the quest and the very modest results? The merit of the encounter was that each side represented a point of reference and orientation for the

215

other. Present need, moral and existential, gave the dialogue its significance. Both sides, each in its own way, were still caught up in the consequences of the Holocaust and trying to cope with them. We were linked together in a way that bordered on the limits of intellectual and emotional expression. The abyss of the past hovered between us and somehow bound us, the one who belonged to the camp of the perpetrators, the other whose allegiance was to victims: we had both become part of a horrible event that was beyond our comprehension.

It is a well-known truth that a man generally encounters the people he wants to meet. For the Germans with moral sensitivity with whom I came into contact, Auschwitz was a still smoldering issue. They evoked from me a rather disturbing feeling: compassion. It was sobering, indeed, to think about a new generation of Germans—and about many of the older ones—who personally *were* morally innocent, who recoiled in horror at the idea of killing Jews (or Gypsies, or Russians or anybody else), and who now had to cope with such a heritage. For them not only was Auschwitz the "past that does not pass." These Germans seemed condemned to live with Auschwitz as an ineradicable nightmare.

Although this process of dialogue left me on less than stable ground, both intellectually and emotionally, it also led to some general conclusions that today seem to me quite clear. Germans and Jews are living today within their own spiritual and social boundaries, are driven by almost unrelated dynamics. Both sides are moved not only by what happened decades ago, but more significantly by the continuing impact of the past on many aspects of their lives. At present, there is a Jewish issue and there is a German issue. They touch, but each has its own sense.

For us Jews, the vital matter is to rebuild our shattered structures and move on. Within that framework, it is indispensable to understand all the implications of the disaster that befell the Jewish people in mid-century, all of them. We should not forget that the Catastrophe had a broader, worrisome European background, although the Germans were its immediate perpetrators. From the German point of view, it seems the principal difficulty is understanding more clearly—in order to cope more effectively with—the dark forces and destructive potentialities that lurk in the complex labyrinth of the German national identity. Dialogue between individuals—clearheaded, unsentimental, yet personal—may well establish a more positive dimension in the Jewish-German understanding.

∾

It took me time to sort out the sequence of thoughts I have described here. Only after I returned to Israel did the diverse levels of my year in Germany begin to come together in my mind: the apparently uncomplicated day-to-day Heidelberg life, the personal experiences, the inner trip down that rocky river of my reflections.

How amazing that year had been! I pondered it while walking with my German friend through the old Jewish cemetery in Worms. Nine hundred years of Jewish existence in Germany lay buried there. A whole dimension of Jewish life and culture, the Ashkenazi branch, had been created in German lands and later carried throughout the world. Some of the greatest creations in modern Jewish history had resulted from the Jewish-German encounter and some of the worst instincts in the German people had been aroused by the Jewish presence in their midst. Now it was a finished chapter. But what a chapter!

I stood in the old cemetery in Worms, and meditated on the end of it all. In a limited way, I too, symbolized that end: I had been born in Germany, German had been my first tongue, but German I was not. Somehow, a second German chapter in my life had opened, and now it was closing. Once again, in a narrow, or perhaps not so narrow sense, I had "moved" to another country, one closely related to the circumstances of my life. It had been a momentous experience, with powerful intellectual and personal dimensions.

Where had my pursuit led me? Regarding the German-Jewish tragedy, I was forced to admit that I understood it even less well than I did before. Apparently, it may happen that the closer one gets to a certain environment, the harder it is to grasp the more general patterns that mold and move that society. I had developed a more reflective attitude toward Germans as a people, and with some Germans I had achieved a very close relationship. I had also learned what a powerful concoction the blend of intellectual query and intimate bond is apt to be, and how volatile; how carefully it must be handled, how impossible are the odds against it. Here, too, I ended up achieving peace with myself, but it was a very sober peace.

In the long run, where had all this left me? Ageless Jewish experience teaches that time unravels quests that our comprehension or our senses are unable to cope with. Remembrance remains, but time softens their rough edges.

∾

In the summer of 1990 I returned to Israel. The Land burned under the sun, but nights in Jerusalem were cool and silent. Jerusalem accepted me back with that aloof toleration of hers: another one with a peculiar story and odd pursuits.

Life moved on. A war was brewing in the Persian Gulf. Hundreds of thousands of new Jewish immigrants were arriving. I was home again. Everything was starting anew, once more.

26

The Phantoms

When I look back, I feel a certain uneasiness. Phantoms from the past arise and distract me. When one has enjoyed several lives, in several environments, different periods run together. Their beginnings and endings overlap. Mixed shadows of impressions and perceptions remain.

Some of these impressions may no longer have much explicit significance—was that not one of the lessons of my visit, decades later, to Chemnitz, the town of my birth? Or to Brazil, the country of my youth? But what about human contacts, past friendships, loves and hatreds? They do not go away, those phantoms. Frequently they conjure up a very private smile. Sometimes they evoke vague or not so vague qualms, sudden recollections of errors committed, pangs of sins conveniently—too conveniently—forgotten. Mostly, they are like fleeting question marks, those ghosts. They pass through my mind as birds through the sky. Sometimes their number increases and they cover the whole horizon of my consciousness.

These phantoms are not threatening. On the contrary, mostly they sing sweetly in my ears. They sing and sing. Are they trying to tell me something? Are they trying to direct me somewhere—or away from something? I keep listening, but in the end I recoil. One must be careful not to be engulfed by that most alluring of all quicksands, memory.

∾

It takes time and patience to handle the delicate interplay between memory and memoir. Memory is anchored in the past; a memoir, I believe now, derives its inner sense and consequently its structure from one's present time and our current concerns.

The casualness of the story told here disquiets me, when I tie it all together. Blind chance has played too large a role in my life. Indeed, except for my emigration to Israel, almost everything important that has happened to me was accidental: that we managed to escape from Germany in 1939, that in Israel I found my way to an academic career in Jewish history. I once spoke about all this with my mother, who in her nineties remained as sharp-minded as always. Had it ever occurred to her, when I was a youngster in São Paulo, stumbling through my troubled teens, that one day I might be a university professor in Jerusalem? Never, she answered, it was beyond any possible guess, indeed, against any sensible logic.

Was there nothing beyond chance? Is there no broader, impersonal pattern within whose matrix my life has taken place? In fact, there is such a pattern of events, as I hope I have demonstrated. Those two great landmarks in twentieth-century Jewish history—the destruction of European Jewry and the establishment of Israel—were major influences in the lives of millions of Jews, I among them. Sometimes the threads binding my own development to those events were obvious and clear-cut, but most often they were almost invisible.

The connections were seldom discernible at first glance. The Holocaust and Jewish statehood were forces essentially antipodal in our Jewish fate. One pointed toward ruin and darkness, the other toward continuity and creation. Both were all-encompassing, and their mutual polarization forced Jews, as individuals and as a society, to pause, ponder and take a stand. At this critical point, personal destiny came up against historical occurrence; the two having touched, a directive emerged with the full poignancy of a moral message.

For me, the major lesson evolving from the present story,

adding significance to the narrative, is how important it is for us—my generation, the generation of our children—to move forward. How dangerous it is for us to remain fixed on the disaster that befell us Jews in the forties, whose long shadow still encumbers our steps—as a society, as individuals—in a thousand subtle ways. Too many of us remain mired in that past, because of our upbringing, our sentiment, or even our personal interest, or because it is so difficult to muster the personal and collective strength to deal with it. True, the Holocaust cannot be forgotten: we are as we are because of it. We carry in us its signs and its consequences even if we are unaware of them, even if we try to forget it all. But life continues: this is for me the meaning of Jewish statehood, of Israel—for Jews in general and for me personally. Whatever the events and circumstances of human existence, sometimes beautiful, sometimes cruel, life goes on.

Life goes on also for my own generation. We have been tossed back and forth so often that many of us have gotten into the habit of dislocation, and have become unable to settle down anywhere. In many cases we became the second generation of Jews wandering from place to place, from environment to environment, from one culture to a second, to a third. Sometimes I find myself wondering if our children will be able to slow down. Arthur Koestler's statement, back in 1949, that with the creation of the Jewish state the Wandering Jew had arrived at the end of his journey, seems no more than wishful thinking. There are some journeys, inner journeys of the collective soul, that do not end at a certain point, or with a given generation. There are journeys that were initiated back in history and may never come to a close.

My own rootlessness, so typical of my generation, is a condition I have come to accept without bitterness. True, from a relatively early age one of my conscious objectives had been to find what is called roots, normalcy. Today I recognize that the effort was doomed to failure from the moment I formulated it as a conscious aim. However, I do not think that my situation has dulled my senses, or made me unhappier than other people I have known. If anything, rootlessness has made my life quite interesting.

Yet theoretically, at least, it seems a tough proposition: is man basically alone, inwardly estranged? What rules, in such a case, should direct his feelings, his behavior, his relationships? What aims should shape his life? I do not have an answer. Furthermore, I have become increasingly distrustful of people who claim they do.

Can it be that the kind of life I have described, my own and that of others not unlike me, points to a pattern which may become more general in the coming years? Recent events in Europe seem to justify my postulate. My latest experiences there have shown me the power of the integrational pull in Western Europe. It appears to me—and may time prove me right—that Europeans are on their way to becoming more European, that is, less German, or French, or Dutch or anything else. Europeans less motivated by nationalistic jealousies and interests? It seems a laudable proposition, past miseries considered. But the price? With growing economic and political interdependence, open frontiers and free contact between individuals and cultures, what will be the spiritual and cultural face of these new Europeans? Around which specific feelings will these new French, or Italians or Germans—or Jews—structure their awareness about themselves as individuals and as societies?

Could it be that a new kind of rootlessness may be the emotional cost of these expanded horizons? Could it be that my generation, although driven by its specific historical circumstances, carrying the burden of its particular destiny, represents the first expression of a situation which larger sections of mankind are going to experience in the future or may already be tasting in the present? Perhaps. If so, our situation would take on an additional meaning: we constitute the beginnings of a human condition whose full significance may yet be revealed in the days to come.

Thanks Are Due To

STAN CHYET, who proved again the old saying that few things are as precious as a good friend.

NUNHO FALBEL, with whom I shared that unique experience, the Zionist youth movement.

YOSSI SHATZMILLER, with whom I shared another great experience, the Hebrew University of Jerusalem.

BARUCH EYAL, remembering happy Beer Sheva days.

JEHUDA REINHARZ, for the many matters (and many people) we have laughed about together.

MARIANNE MEYER-KRAMER, who listened and understood.

EIKE WOLGAST, remembering, among many other events, how we walked up to the fortress of Massada, in the Judean desert.

SYLVIA FUKS-FRIED, who brought me to ponder that common sense is very much of a moral category.

ANNE MARIE and JOE SANDLER, who helped at a critical moment.

SANDRA WILLIAMSON, who undertook the Herculean job of cleaning the stables of my English grammar.

The people of Wayne State University Press, and particularly ARTHUR EVANS, KATHY WILDFONG, ALICE NIGOGHOSIAN, and STACY LIEBERMAN, who, from the perspective of the author, knew how to turn a professional job into a most pleasant experience.

RUTH and EDITH, who accompanied much of the way here described.

NOA, HILLEL and OFRA, who supported more than they are aware of.

And thanks to little HAMUTAL, Amnon and Noa's daughter, who thinks that I am a very funny *saba*, but a bit weird—and is that child right . . .

INDEX